Warman's

fiesta

Identification and Price Guide

Glen Victorey

©2007 Krause Publications

Published by

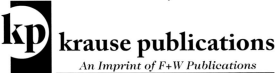

An Imprint of F+W Publications

**700 East State Street • Iola, WI 54990-0001
715-445-2214 • 888-457-2873
www.krausebooks.com**

Library of Congress Control Number: 2007922998
ISBN-13: 978-0-89689-557-7
ISBN-10: 0-89689-557-2

Designed by Marilyn McGrane
Edited by Mary Sieber

Printed in China

Acknowledgments

Thank you to all the wonderful Fiesta fanatics out there whose paths have crossed with mine over the past 25 years of my involvement with this tableware.

Several people have contributed to the content of this book. I'd like to thank:

Mark Chervenka, who did a great job writing about the fakes and frauds of the Fiesta world.

James and Marlene Hintz, who helped pack up much of the vintage Fiesta photographed in this book, drive three hours for a photo shoot, unpack, repack, and drive back. We did this on three different snowy winter days. Thanks!

And to Nancy Sierszen, a friend who gave me some of her family's Fiesta, thereby setting into motion a search that has continued over these last 25 years.

About the Author

Glen Victorey has been a collector since fifth grade when he began collecting trading cards with his brother, Tom. From that beginning, it was only a small step to collecting *TV Guide* magazines, lunch boxes, and beer and soft drink cans. In 1981, a friend was cleaning out her home and gave him a partial set of Fiesta. In a short time it was clear that a major addiction had been born. Victorey resides in Milwaukee, where he works in the party industry. Like so many others, Glen and his brother have never forgiven their parents for throwing out all their trading cards and other good stuff!

Contents

On the Road to Fiesta

The Homer Laughlin China Company originated with a two-kiln pottery on the banks of the Ohio River in East Liverpool, Ohio. Built in 1873-'74 by Homer Laughlin and his brother, Shakespeare, the firm was first known as the Ohio Valley Pottery, and later Laughlin Bros. Pottery. It was one of the first white-ware plants in the country.

After a tentative beginning, the company was awarded a prize for having the best white-ware at the 1876 Centennial Exposition in Philadelphia.

Three years later, Shakespeare sold his interest in the business to Homer, who continued on until 1897. At that time, Homer Laughlin sold his interest in the newly incorporated firm to a group of investors, including Charles, Louis, and Marcus Aaron and the company bookkeeper, William E. Wells.

Under new ownership in 1907, the headquarters and a new 30-kiln plant were built across the Ohio River in Newell, West Virginia, the present manufacturing and headquarters location.

In the 1920s, two additions to the Homer Laughlin staff set the stage for the company's greatest success: the Fiesta line.

Dr. Albert V. Bleininger was hired in 1920. A scientist, author, and educator, he oversaw the conversion from bottle kilns to the more efficient tunnel kilns.

In 1927, the company hired designer Frederick Hurten Rhead, a member of a distinguished family of English ceramists. Having previously worked at Weller Pottery and Roseville Pottery, Rhead began to develop the artistic quality of the company's wares, and to experiment with shapes and glazes. In 1935, this work culminated in his designs for the Fiesta line.

Doorway into the Homer Laughlin China Company in Newell, West Virginia:
"Through these portals pass the best potters in the world."

Fiesta Colors

From 1936 to 1972, Fiesta was produced in 14 colors (other than special promotions). These colors are usually divided into the "original colors" of cobalt blue, light green, ivory, red, turquoise, and yellow (cobalt blue, light green, red, and yellow only on the Kitchen Kraft line, introduced in 1939); the "1950s colors" of chartreuse, forest green, gray, and rose (introduced in 1951); medium green (introduced in 1959); plus the later additions of Casuals, Amberstone, Fiesta Ironstone, and Casualstone ("Coventry") in antique gold, mango red, and turf green; and the striped, decal, and Lustre pieces. No Fiesta was produced from 1973 to 1985. The colors that make up the "original" and "1950s" groups are sometimes referred to as "the standard 11."

In many pieces, medium green is the hardest to find and the most expensive Fiesta color.

FIESTA COLORS AND YEARS OF PRODUCTION UP TO 1972

ANTIQUE GOLD—DARK BUTTERSCOTCH (1969-1972)

MANGO RED—SAME AS ORIGINAL RED (1970-1972)

CHARTREUSE—YELLOWISH GREEN (1951-1959)

MEDIUM GREEN—BRIGHT RICH GREEN (1959-1969)

COBALT BLUE—DARK OR "ROYAL" BLUE (1936-1951)

RED—REDDISH ORANGE (1936-1944 AND 1959-1972)

FOREST GREEN—DARK "HUNTER" GREEN (1951-1959)

ROSE—DUSTY, DARK ROSE (1951-1959)

GRAY—LIGHT OR ASH GRAY (1951-1959)

TURF GREEN—OLIVE (1969-1972)

GREEN—OFTEN CALLED LIGHT GREEN WHEN COMPARING IT TO OTHER GREEN GLAZES, ALSO CALLED "ORIGINAL" GREEN (1936-1951)

TURQUOISE—SKY BLUE, LIKE THE STONE (1937-1969)

IVORY—CREAMY, SLIGHTLY YELLOWED (1936-1951)

YELLOW—GOLDEN YELLOW (1936-1969)

Dimensions and Colors

Even though we have provided detailed dimensions for each Fiesta piece, the nature of the machinery used to make each item, and the skill of the potters who applied some details by hand, result in variations throughout the line.

Some glazes also have several shades, to the point that even seasoned collectors and antiques dealers may mistake an especially heavy light green glaze for the more rare medium green. Some glazes are also prone to mottling, including turquoise and—to a lesser degree—red. Cobalt blue and turf green pieces tend to show even the slightest scratches more obviously than lighter glazes, and ivory examples often exhibit cloudy, yellowish, or sooty spots along rims and bases.

Keep in mind that Fiesta colors will also look different depending on the light at hand. Incandescent, fluorescent, and natural light will each add a different color element.

Editor's Note: Every effort was made to ensure that the photographs in this book present the Fiesta line in its proper colors. Slight differences in the color of the glazes used when the Fiesta items were produced, as well as the quality of some of the images, may distort the color of some pieces pictured in this book.

The Red Scare

During World War II, the U.S. government restricted the use of uranium oxide, which gave Fiesta red its color. This restriction was not lifted until 1959. Though the company then used a different formulation for the red glaze, people were still concerned about vintage glazes with even a minute uranium or heavy metal content. The Food and Drug Administration had previously determined that daily use of vintage dinnerware as serving pieces does not pose a hazard, as long as the glazes and decals were properly applied and fired. To be on the safe side, avoid storing foods that contain a high level of acid, such as tomato products, sauerkraut, and vinegar-based products, in any vintage Fiesta pieces. Also, do not use vintage Fiesta in a microwave oven.

Bottom Marks

Bottom of 6" bread plate in turquoise, showing "Genuine Fiesta" stamp.

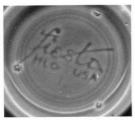

Bottom of No. 1 mixing bowl in green, showing sagger pin marks, the "Fiesta/HLCo. USA" impressed mark, and the faint "1" size indicator. The impressed size mark on the bottom of the No. 2 mixing bowl in yellow is too faint to be seen in this image.

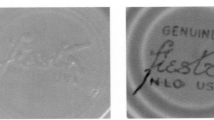

Bottom of a teacup saucer in turquoise, showing sagger pin marks and the "Genuine Fiesta" stamp.

An ink stamp on the bottom of a piece of Fiesta.

Examples of impressed Fiesta bottom marks.

Notice the different bottoms of two ashtrays. The left one has a set of rings with no room for a logo. The right ashtray has rings along the outer edge, opposite of the ring pattern on the ashtray above. The red example is an older example. The yellow ashtray with the logo can be dated to a time period after 1940.

Two different impressed marks on the bottoms of relish tray inserts.

Fiesta pieces were glazed on the underside, so before being fired, each piece was placed on a stilt to keep it off the floor of the kiln. The stilt was made up of three sagger pins positioned an equal distance from each other to form three points of a triangle. If you inspect the underside of any piece of Fiesta, which has a completely glazed bottom, you will notice three small blemishes in a triangular pattern. Later in Fiesta's production run, the undersides of pieces were glazed and then wiped, creating a dry foot, before going into the kiln to be fired.

A 9" cobalt blue plate rests on a stilt with sagger pins to show the basic idea of how it worked. Please note that this stilt is not the exact one that would have been used by Homer Laughlin China Company, but rather an updated style in use today by many ceramic studios.

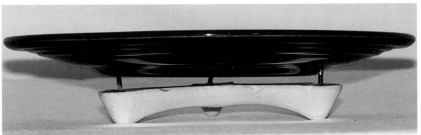

Color Timeline

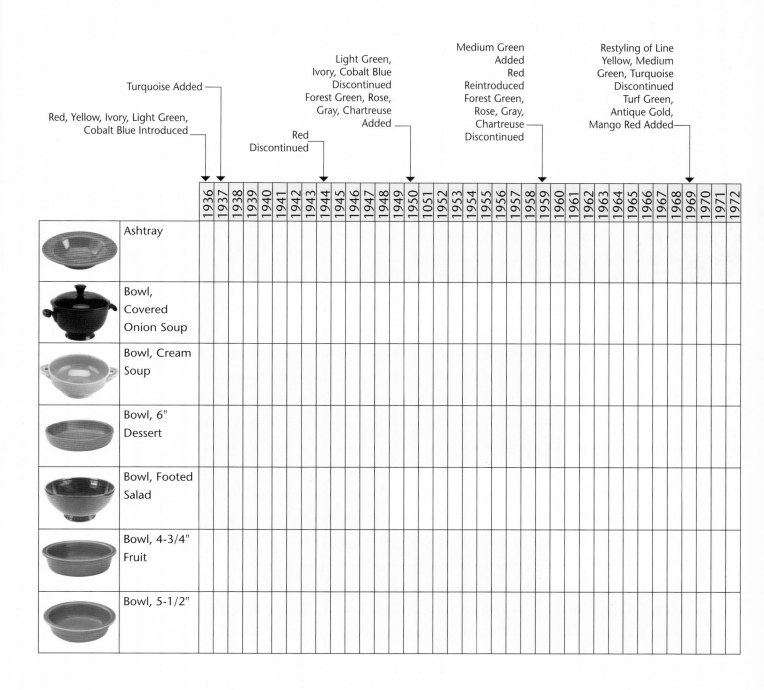

Red, Yellow, Ivory, Light Green, Cobalt Blue Introduced

Turquoise Added

Red Discontinued

Light Green, Ivory, Cobalt Blue Discontinued Forest Green, Rose, Gray, Chartreuse Added

Medium Green Added Red Reintroduced Forest Green, Rose, Gray, Chartreuse Discontinued

Restyling of Line Yellow, Medium Green, Turquoise Discontinued Turf Green, Antique Gold, Mango Red Added

Ashtray

Bowl, Covered Onion Soup

Bowl, Cream Soup

Bowl, 6" Dessert

Bowl, Footed Salad

Bowl, 4-3/4" Fruit

Bowl, 5-1/2"

	1936	1937	1938	1939	1940	1941	1942	1943	1944	1945	1946	1947	1948	1949	1950	1051	1952	1953	1954	1955	1956	1957	1958	1959	1960	1961	1962	1963	1964	1965	1966	1967	1968	1969	1970	1971	1972
Bowl, 11-3/4"																																					
Bowl, Individual Salad																																					
Bowl, #1-#7 Nested Mixing																																					
Bowl Lids, Mixing																																					
Bowl, 8-1/2" Nappy																																					
Bowl, 9-1/2" Nappy																																					
Candleholder, Bulb																																					
Candleholder, Tripod																																					
Carafe																																					
Casserole																																					

		1936	1937	1938	1939	1940	1941	1942	1943	1944	1945	1946	1947	1948	1949	1950	1051	1952	1953	1954	1955	1956	1957	1958	1959	1960	1961	1962	1963	1964	1965	1966	1967	1968	1969	1970	1971	1972
	Coffeepot																																					
	Coffeepot, Demitasse																																					
	Comport																																					
	Comport, Sweets																																					
	Creamer, Ring-Handle																																					
	Creamer, Stick-Handle																																					
	Sugar Bowl																																					
	Demitasse Cup & Saucer																																					
	Eggcup																																					
	Teacut & Saucer																																					

fiesta Color Timeline

		1936	1937	1938	1939	1940	1941	1942	1943	1944	1945	1946	1947	1948	1949	1950	1051	1952	1953	1954	1955	1956	1957	1958	1959	1960	1961	1962	1963	1964	1965	1966	1967	1968	1969	1970	1971	1972
	Tom & Jerry Mug																																					
	Marmalade Jar																																					
	Mustard Jar																																					
	Pitcher, Disk Water																																					
	Pitcher, Ice																																					
	Pitcher, Syrup																																					
	Two-Pint Jug																																					
	Plate, 6"																																					
	Plate, 7"																																					
	Plate, 9"																																					

		1936	1937	1938	1939	1940	1941	1942	1943	1944	1945	1946	1947	1948	1949	1950	1051	1952	1953	1954	1955	1956	1957	1958	1959	1960	1961	1962	1963	1964	1965	1966	1967	1968	1969	1970	1971	1972
	Plate, 10"																																					
	Plate, Cake																																					
	Plate, 13" Chop																																					
	Plate, 15" Chop																																					
	Plate, 10-1/2" Compartment																																					
	Plate, 12" Compartment																																					
	Plate, Deep																																					
	Platter																																					
	Salt & Pepper Shakers																																					
	Sauceboat																																					

fiesta   Color Timeline

		1936	1937	1938	1939	1940	1941	1942	1943	1944	1945	1946	1947	1948	1949	1950	1051	1952	1953	1954	1955	1956	1957	1958	1959	1960	1961	1962	1963	1964	1965	1966	1967	1968	1969	1970	1971	1972
	Teapot, Medium																																					
	Teapot, Large																																					
	Tray, Relish																																					
	Tray, Utility																																					
	Tumbler, Water																																					
	Vase, Bud																																					
	Vase, 8"																																					
	Vase, 10"																																					
	Vase, 12"																																					

Promotional Items		1936	1937	1938	1939	1940	1941	1942	1943	1944	1945	1946	1947	1948	1949	1950	1051	1952	1953	1954	1955	1956	1957	1958	1959	1960	1961	1962	1963	1964	1965	1966	1967	1968	1969	1970	1971	1972
	Unlisted Salad Bowl																																					
	Casserole With Pie Plate																																					
	French Casserole																																					
	Creamer/ Sugar/Tray Set																																					
	Disk Juice Pitcher																																					
	Juice Tumbler																																					
	Chop Plate With Handle																																					
	Refrigerator Stacking Set																																					

How Prices Were Determined

Determining fair market values to be published in books on collectibles is always difficult. There are many schools of thought on this matter.

Do you take every Fiesta 7" ivory plate offered for sale over the past year, average the prices, and come up with a standard secondary market value?

Many people buy collectibles using online auctions. This can go either way in terms of the price you end up paying. For instance, you may have people from all over the world vying for one item. Timing is also critical. The time of the year in which the auction is conducted, how long it runs, the time of day it ends, and the number of duplicate items being offered for sale at the same time all contribute to the final selling price.

Online auctions, as well as live auctions, antiques and collectibles stores, flea markets, and shows were all surveyed to arrive at the secondary market values published in this book. This pricing reflects Fiesta items in **mint condition** only. Any items with chips, severe scratches, dings, cracks, etc., are 50%-60% *less than* the value listed.

Become a detective when looking for a new addition to your collection. Nearly everyone has a story of buying what he or she thought was a great piece, only to find out later that it was damaged.

When buying one part of a multiple-piece item, such as a lid without a bottom or a relish tray insert without the rest of the tray, *beware*. The color and/or size may be slightly off. A relish tray insert may not be an exact fit. Lids are usually harder to find than bottoms. Expect to pay about 55%-60% of the total price for a top alone.

The values in this book represent the most fair and accurate pricing at press time.

Happy collecting!

In the early years of Fiesta's development, Homer Laughlin China Company Art Director Frederick Rhead designed many pieces that for one reason or another were never put into production. One of the rarest is the two-cup teapot (also called the individual teapot), which reportedly garnered the highest price ever paid for a piece of Fiesta. At an auction conducted by Strawser Auctions of Wolcottville, Indiana, on Sept. 12, 2004, this rare piece—believed by some to be one of only three known to exist—sold for **$20,075**.

Photo courtesy Strawser Auctions

Vintage Fiesta Pieces

Ashtrays

In a time when smoking was common at dinner parties, Homer Laughlin, along with other dinnerware manufacturers of the period, produced ashtrays to go along with their lines. In fact, many companies produced "smoking sets" to appeal to men, as either a purchase for themselves or as a gift, thereby expanding the marketability of the line.

There are two bottom variations known. Before 1940, the ashtray base has seven rings and is not marked; after 1940, the base has two rings and a "Genuine Fiesta" stamp. Production of red examples was halted in 1944 and resumed in 1959.

DEGREE OF DIFFICULTY

1 for all colors other than medium green, which ranks 3.

DIMENSIONS:

7-1/2" by 8-3/4" by 5"

PRODUCTION DATES:

1938 to 1969

COLORS		1950s COLORS	
Cobalt Blue	$50-$59	Chartreuse	$69-$79
Ivory	$50-$59	Forest Green	$79-$89
Light Green	$42-$48	Gray	$72-$79
Red	$65-$72	Rose	$72-$80
Turquoise	$44-$50		
Yellow	$39-$45	Medium Green	$195-$215

Ashtray in red. **$65-$72**

Ashtray in cobalt blue. **$50-$59**

Ashtray in medium green. Sold at auction in October 2006 for **$100.**

Photo courtesy Strawser Auctions

Ashtray in forest green. Sold at auction in October 2006 for **$30.**

Photo courtesy Strawser Auctions

Ashtray in rose. Sold at auction in October 2006 for **$45.**

Photo courtesy Strawser Auctions

Ashtray in ivory. **$50-$59**

Ashtray in yellow. **$39-$45**

Ashtray in light green. **$42-$48**

VINTAGE FIESTA PIECES

Stack of four ashtrays in red, cobalt blue, ivory and yellow.

Ashtray in light green, **$42-$48,** with yellow eggcup.

Four ashtrays in yellow, red, ivory, and cobalt blue.

Notice the different bottoms of two ashtrays. The left has a set of rings with no room for a logo. The one on the right has rings along the outer edge, opposite of the ring pattern on the ashtray at left.

Bowls

Covered onion soup bowl

An item that was commonplace among 1930s dinnerware was an onion soup bowl with cover. For whatever reason (price, styling, etc.), they did not sell well in the approximately two years they were in production. Because of this, covered onion soup bowls are hard to find. Expect to pay a premium price for a rare turquoise example as the bowls were discontinued at about the same time that the turquoise glaze was introduced.

DEGREE OF DIFFICULTY

3 for colors other than turquoise, which ranks 5+.

DIMENSIONS:

6-1/8" by 4-1/2" by 4-3/8" tall with lid

PRODUCTION DATES:

1936 to late 1937

COLORS

Cobalt Blue	$680-$739
Ivory	$710-$729
Light Green	$640-$675
Red	$695-$735
Yellow	$635-$695
Turquoise	$7,500-$8,000

Covered onion soup bowl in ivory. **$710-$729**

Covered onion soup bowl in light green. **$640-$675**

Rare covered onion soup bowl in turquoise with minor glaze miss to rim of lid. Sold at auction in October 2006 for **$3,100.**

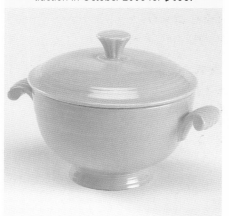

Covered onion soup bowl in red. Sold at auction in October 2006 for **$400.**

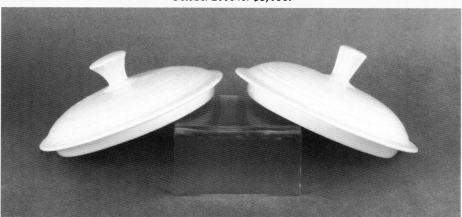

Covered onion soup bowl in yellow.
$635-$695

Two covered onion soup bowls and lids in ivory. The lid on the left is the typical production style with a more flared knob and shorter flange ring; the lid on the right is the early production style and has a more tapered knob and deeper flange ring. The more common one on the left is valued at **$710-$729.** There is no established value for the one on the right.

Covered onion soup bowl in cobalt blue.
$680-$739

VINTAGE FIESTA PIECES

Cream soup cup

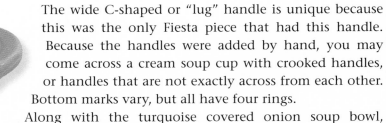

The wide C-shaped or "lug" handle is unique because this was the only Fiesta piece that had this handle. Because the handles were added by hand, you may come across a cream soup cup with crooked handles, or handles that are not exactly across from each other. Bottom marks vary, but all have four rings.

Along with the turquoise covered onion soup bowl, a medium green cream soup is the centerpiece of any Fiesta collection. Having been withdrawn from production at about the same time as the medium green color was introduced, cream soup bowls in this color command a hefty price. Production of red examples was halted in 1944 and resumed in 1959.

DEGREE OF DIFFICULTY

1-2 for colors other than medium green, which ranks 5+.

DIMENSIONS:

6-5/8" by 5-1/16" by 2-1/4" tall

PRODUCTION DATES:

1936 until 1959

ORIGINAL COLORS		1950S COLORS	
Cobalt Blue	$54-$65	Chartreuse	$62-$70
Ivory	$52-$62	Forest Green	$65-$74
Light Green	$44-$50	Gray	$61-$72
Red	$58-$70	Rose	$62-$73
Turquoise	$43-$49		
Yellow	$41-$47	Medium Green	$4,225-$4,449

Cream soup cup in chartreuse. Sold at auction in October 2006 for **$35.**

Cream soup cup group in six original colors: red, cobalt blue, ivory, turquoise, light green, and yellow. Sold at auction in October 2006 for **$185.**

VINTAGE FIESTA PIECES

Cream soup cup in gray. **$61-$72**

Cream soup cup in rose.
Sold at auction in October 2006 for **$40.**

Cream soup cup in cobalt blue.
Sold at auction in October 2006 for **$25.**

Cream soup cup in forest green with metal
holder and spoon. Sold at auction in October
2006 for **$225.**

Cream soup cups in ivory, **$52-$62**, turquoise, **$43-$49**, and red, **$58-$70.**

Cream soup cup in turquoise. **$43-$49**

VINTAGE FIESTA PIECES

fiesta   Dessert bowl

Examples can be found with either four or five interior rings. You may also find bowls with an unglazed foot, although most examples are glazed, complete with the three marks where the piece came in contact with the sagger pins. Production of red examples was halted in 1944 and resumed in 1959.

DEGREE OF DIFFICULTY

1 for the original six colors;
2 for the 1950s colors;
and 4-5 for medium green.

DIMENSIONS:

6-1/4" by 1-1/4"

PRODUCTION DATES:

1936 until late 1960

ORIGINAL COLORS		1950S COLORS	
Cobalt Blue	$40-$50	Chartreuse	$46-$51
Ivory	$41-$50	Forest Green	$46-$51
Light Green	$36-$42	Gray	$45-$52
Red	$42-$52	Rose	$45-$55
Turquoise	$35-$45		
Yellow	$34-$45	Medium Green	$675-$748

Dessert bowls in cobalt blue, **$40-$50**, red, **$42-$52**, and turquoise, **$35-$45**.

Dessert bowl in yellow. **$34-$45**

Dessert bowl in rose. **$45-$55**

Dessert bowl in ivory. **$41-$50**

Dessert bowl in chartreuse. **$46-$51**

Dessert bowl in forest green. **$46-$51**

Dessert bowl in gray. **$45-$52**

Dessert bowls in six original colors.

Dessert bowl in medium green. **$675-$748**

Dessert bowl in turquoise. **$35-$45**

Dessert bowl in red. **$42-$52**

Dessert bowl in cobalt blue. **$40-$50**

Dessert bowls in turquoise, **$35-$45,** light green, **$36-$42,** and red, **$42-$52.**

fiesta Footed Salad bowl

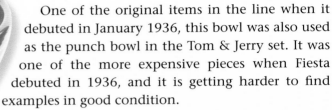

One of the original items in the line when it debuted in January 1936, this bowl was also used as the punch bowl in the Tom & Jerry set. It was one of the more expensive pieces when Fiesta debuted in 1936, and it is getting harder to find examples in good condition.

Variations on this bowl include the foot that was applied by different techniques, leaving it either thick or thin, and two different back stamps, either ink stamped or in-mold. Production of red examples was halted in 1944.

DEGREE OF DIFFICULTY

3-4

DIMENSIONS:

11-3/8" by 5-1/2"

PRODUCTION DATES:

1936 to 1946

COLORS

Cobalt Blue	**$410-$460**
Ivory	**$385-$445**
Light Green	**$387-$395**
Red	**$415-$475**
Turquoise	**$387-$399**
Yellow	**$375-$395**

Footed salad bowl in turquoise. Sold at auction in October 2006 for **$375.**

Photo courtesy Strawser Auctions

Footed salad bowl in red. **$415-$475**

VINTAGE FIESTA PIECES

Footed salad bowl in yellow. **$375-$395**

Footed salad bowl in ivory. **$385-$445**

Footed salad bowl in cobalt blue. **$410-$460**

VINTAGE FIESTA PIECES

fiesta   4-3/4" Fruit bowl

Due to its long production run, there are several variations in the number of rings as well as the size of the rings inside the bowl. The other variation (except in medium green) is on the underside of this piece. Early examples were completely glazed so you will find sagger pin marks—three equally spaced on the bottom. Later bowls have a wiped foot. The 4-3/4" fruit bowl was in production for almost 25 years, so it is rather easy to find. The exception is a medium green example. Production of red examples was halted in 1944 and resumed in 1959.

DEGREE OF DIFFICULTY

1-2 for colors other than medium green, which ranks 4-5.

DIMENSIONS:

4-3/4" by 1-1/2"

PRODUCTION DATES:

1936 to late 1959

ORIGINAL COLORS		1950S COLORS	
Cobalt Blue	$27-$32	Chartreuse	$32-$36
Ivory	$28-$32	Forest Green	$33-$37
Light Green	$25-$30	Gray	$30-$35
Red	$31-$33	Rose	$30-$37
Turquoise	$23-$29		
Yellow	$23-$27	Medium Green	$610-$665

4-3/4" fruit bowl (bottom right) in medium green. **$610-$665**

4-3/4" fruit bowl group in all six original colors: red, cobalt blue, ivory, turquoise, light green, and yellow. Sold at auction in October 2006 for **$90.**

Photo courtesy Strawser Auctions

4-3/4" fruit bowls in chartreuse, **$32-$36,** forest green, **$33-$37,** turquoise, **$23-$29,** ivory, **$28-$32,** and yellow, **$23-$27.**

Photo courtesy Strawser Auctions

4-3/4" fruit bowl group of four in rose, gray, forest green, and chartreuse. Sold at auction in October 2006 for **$55.**

Light green fruit bowls, one 4-3/4" and the other 5-1/2", showing the variation in color intensity and ring patterns.

4-3/4" fruit bowl in cobalt blue. **$27-$32**

4-3/4" fruit bowl in ivory. **$28-$32**

4-3/4" fruit bowl in yellow. **$23-$27**

4-3/4" fruit bowl in red. **$31-$33**

4-3/4" Fruit bowl

4-3/4" fruit bowl in light green. **$25-$30**

4-3/4" fruit bowl in turquoise. **$23-$29**

Fruit bowls in turquoise, **$23-$29,** cobalt blue, **$27-$32,** red, **$31-$33,** ivory, **$28-$32,** yellow, **$23-$27,** and light green, **$25-$30.**

fiesta   5-1/2" Fruit bowl

5-1/2" fruit bowls in turquoise, **$23-$30**, ivory, **$27-$34**, and light green, **$24-$31**.

Both this bowl and the 4-3/4" fruit bowl are scaled-down versions of the 8-1/2" and 9-1/2" nappies. The variations on this bowl are the same as the ones on its smaller sibling, the 4-3/4" fruit bowl. This is a great piece with many uses, including as a candy or nut dish, along with a small oatmeal bowl. Production of red examples was halted in 1944 and resumed in 1959.

DEGREE OF DIFFICULTY

1 for the original colors;
2 for the 1950s colors; and
3 for medium green.

DIMENSIONS:

5-1/2" by 1-3/4"

PRODUCTION DATES:

1936 to late 1969

ORIGINAL COLORS		1950S COLORS	
Cobalt Blue	**$26-$35**	Chartreuse	**$32-$39**
Ivory	**$27-$34**	Forest Green	**$32-$40**
Light Green	**$24-$31**	Gray	**$34-$39**
Red	**$27-$35**	Rose	**$33-$39**
Turquoise	**$23-$30**		
Yellow	**$23-$30**	Medium Green	**$65-$72**

5-1/2" fruit bowl in light green, **$24-$31.**

5-1/2" fruit bowl group in all five 1950s colors: medium green, forest green, rose, chartreuse, and gray. Sold at auction in October 2006 for **$90.**

Photo courtesy Strawser Auctions

5-1/2" fruit bowl in chartreuse. **$32-$39**

5-1/2" fruit bowl in red. **$27-$35**

5-1/2" fruit bowl in rose. **$33-$39**

5-1/2" fruit bowl in ivory. **$27-$34**

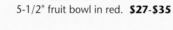

5-1/2" fruit bowl in cobalt blue. **$26-$35**

5-1/2" fruit bowl in turquoise. **$23-$30**

5-1/2" fruit bowl in yellow. **$23-$30**

5-1/2" fruit bowl in forest green. **$32-$40**

5-1/2" fruit bowl in gray. **$34-$39**

VINTAGE FIESTA PIECES

fiesta 11-3/4" Fruit bowl

This bowl was designed by Frederick Rhead to be part of the Kitchen Kraft line. When the bowl was not approved by Homer Laughlin Co. management for the Kitchen Kraft line, it was added to the Fiesta line. You will notice the lack of rings under the flange (lip) of the bowl.

During the 1930s and 1940s, it was common to have a bowl of fruit (usually the waxed variety), along with a pair of candleholders, on a dining room table. This wide and shallow bowl fit the bill. It could also be used as a centerpiece bowl for flowers. Production of red examples was halted in 1944.

DEGREE OF DIFFICULTY

3-4

DIMENSIONS:

11-3/8" by 3

PRODUCTION DATES:

1937 to 1946

COLORS

Cobalt Blue	$295-$340
Ivory	$295-$330
Light Green	$290-$335
Red	$310-$340
Turquoise	$295-$335
Yellow	$280-$315

11-3/4" fruit bowl in light green. **$290-$335**

11-3/4" fruit bowl in cobalt blue. Sold at auction in October 2006 for **$250**.

11-3/4" fruit bowl in red, with factory flaw.
$310-$340

11-3/4" fruit bowl in yellow. **$280-$315**

11-3/4" fruit bowl in ivory. **$295-$330**

11-3/4" fruit bowl in turquoise. Sold at auction in October 2006 for **$150**.

VINTAGE FIESTA PIECES

fiesta Individual salad bowl

The individual salad bowl made its Fiesta debut in 1959, the first new item in the line since 1940. Although Homer Laughlin Co.'s Harlequin line offered a very similar bowl in 1939, it would take 20 years for the company to add it to the Fiesta lineup. Even though the individual salad bowl was produced for approximately 10 years, it is slightly harder to find than other Fiesta bowls. You may find one with no inside rings in the bottom. This may have been due to either the line being updated to the Fiesta Ironstone line or to the fact that the shape was shared with another Homer Laughlin pattern. Marks include the impressed "Fiesta/Made in USA" or the "Genuine Fiesta" stamp.

DEGREE OF DIFFICULTY

2-3

DIMENSIONS:

7-5/8" by 2-3/8"

PRODUCTION DATES:

1959 to 1969

COLORS

Red	**$95-$115**
Turquoise	**$89-$95**
Yellow	**$89-$96**
Medium Green	**$115-$130**

Individual salad bowl in turquoise. **$89-$95**

Individual salad bowl in medium green. **$115-$130**

Individual salad bowl in red. **$95-$115**

Individual salad bowl in yellow. **$89-$96**

The individual salad bowl made its Fiesta debut in 1959, the first new item in the line since 1940.

fiesta

Mixing bowl #1

Production of these bowls lasted approximately 8-1/2 years. Late in 1942 the #1 mixing bowl was available only in red. Bowls made before 1938 have rings inside the bottom, and are usually marked "Fiesta/HLC USA" with the size number. Bowls made later have no rings and are usually marked "Fiesta/Made in USA" with the size number. Part of the selling point of these bowls was that the customer could purchase whichever size bowl was needed. The smallest (#1) and the two largest (#6 and #7) must not have sold well, as they are hardest to find today.

DEGREE OF DIFFICULTY

3-4

DIMENSIONS:

3-1/2" by 5"

PRODUCTION DATES:

1936 to 1944

COLORS

Cobalt Blue	**$275-$295**
Ivory	**$275-$295**
Light Green	**$210-$235**
Red	**$249-$295**
Turquoise	**$275-$299**
Yellow	**$224-$249**

#1 mixing bowl in red, **$249-$295,** with an ivory lid, **$875-$1,000.**

#1 mixing bowl in light green. Sold at auction in October 2006 for **$80.**

Photo courtesy Strawser Auctions

#1 mixing bowl in turquoise. **$275-$299.**

Nested mixing bowls.

fiesta Mixing bowl #2

Late in 1942 this size was available only in yellow. Bowls made before 1938 have rings inside the bottom, and are usually marked "Fiesta/HLC USA." Bowls made later have no rings and are usually marked "Fiesta/Made in USA." Although all seven bowls were originally offered in all six Fiesta colors, after mid-1942, each bowl was only offered in one color.

Photo courtesy Strawser Auctions

#2 mixing bowl in light green. Sold at auction in October 2006 for **$55**.

DEGREE OF DIFFICULTY

2

DIMENSIONS:
4" by 5-7/8"

PRODUCTION DATES:
1936 to 1944

COLORS

Cobalt Blue	$118-$147
Ivory	$127-$156
Light Green	$112-$140
Red	$120-$149
Turquoise	$118-$143
Yellow	$115-$140

#2 mixing bowl in turquoise, **$118-$147**, with a cobalt blue lid.

#2 mixing bowl in cobalt blue. **$118-$147**

#2 mixing bowl in yellow. **$115-$140**

VINTAGE FIESTA PIECES

#3 mixing bowl in red, **$135-$158**, with bowl lid in light green, $800-$900; lids in red, **$900-$1,100**, and yellow, **$800-$900**.

Late in 1942 this size was available only in light green. Bowls made before 1938 have rings inside the bottom, and are usually marked "Fiesta/HLC USA." Bowls made later have no rings and are usually marked "Fiesta/Made in USA." Originally, all seven mixing bowls had rings inside the bottom. During the course of the production run, the bowls lost the inside rings—no doubt making it easier to mix and to clean the bowls.

DEGREE OF DIFFICULTY

2

DIMENSIONS:

4-1/2" by 6-3/4"

PRODUCTION DATES:

1936 to 1944

COLORS

Cobalt Blue	$138-$165
Ivory	$137-$160
Light Green	$122-$145
Red	$135-$158
Turquoise	$130-$155
Yellow	$125-$1505

Photo courtesy Strawser Auctions

#3 mixing bowl in ivory. Sold at auction in October 2006 for **$90**.

#3 mixing bowl, **$125-$150**, and lid in yellow, **$800-$900**.

#3 mixing bowl, **$138-$165**, and lid in cobalt blue, **$900-$1,100**.

#3 mixing bowl in red. **$135-$158**

#4 mixing
bowl in ivory.
$152-$178

Late in 1942 this size was available only in ivory. Bowls made before 1938 have rings inside the bottom, and are usually marked "Fiesta/HLC USA" with the size number. Bowls made later have no rings and are usually marked "Fiesta/Made in USA" with the size number. After approximately five years, the mixing bowls were only available in one color each. Starting with the smallest size (#1), the colors chosen were:

#1	Red	#5	Yellow
#2	Yellow	#6	Turquoise
#3	Light Green	#7	Cobalt Blue
#4	Ivory		

DEGREE OF DIFFICULTY

2

DIMENSIONS:

5" by 7-3/4"

PRODUCTION DATES:

1936 to 1944

COLORS

Cobalt Blue	**$165-$185**
Ivory	**$152-$178**
Light Green	**$127-$153**
Red	**$170-$195**
Turquoise	**$130-$157**
Yellow	**$121-$148**

#4 mixing bowl in cobalt blue. **$165-$185**

#4 mixing bowl in turquoise. **$130-$157**

#4 mixing bowl in light green. Sold at auction in October 2006 for **$50.**

Photo courtesy Strawser Auctions

VINTAGE FIESTA PIECES

Mixing bowl #5

#5 mixing bowl in ivory. **$225-$265**

Late in 1942 this size was available only in yellow. Bowls made before 1938 have rings inside the bottom, and are usually marked "Fiesta/HLC USA" with the size number. Bowls made later have no rings and are usually marked "Fiesta/Made in USA" with the size number. The set of seven bowls are also known as nesting bowls because they fit (or nested) inside each other. A homemaker of the Depression era could store a set of seven bowls in the space it took to store the largest bowl.

DEGREE OF DIFFICULTY

2

DIMENSIONS:

5-3/4" by 8-1/2"

PRODUCTION DATES:

1936 to 1944

COLORS

Cobalt Blue	$249-$260
Ivory	$225-$265
Light Green	$210-$245
Red	$249-$260
Turquoise	$225-$245
Yellow	$195-$210

#5 mixing bowl in cobalt blue. Sold at auction in October 2006 for **$65.**

#5 mixing bowl in turquoise. Sold at auction in October 2006 for **$50.**

#5 mixing bowl in yellow. Sold at auction in October 2006 for **$30.**

Photo courtesy Strawser Auctions

Photo courtesy Strawser Auctions

Photo courtesy Strawser Auctions

#6 mixing bowl in turquoise. Sold at auction in October 2006 for **$190**.

Photo courtesy Strawser Auctions

Late in 1942 this size was available only in turquoise. Bowls made before 1938 have rings inside the bottom, and are usually marked "Fiesta/HLC USA" with the size number. Bowls made later have no rings and are usually marked "Fiesta/Made in USA" with the size number. The smallest (#1) and the two largest (#6 and #7) are the hardest to find of the seven bowls. Because these bowls were each sold individually, a homemaker could buy exactly the size bowl she wanted.

DEGREE OF DIFFICULTY

3

DIMENSIONS:

6-1/4" by 9-3/4"

PRODUCTION DATES:

1936 to 1944

COLORS

Cobalt Blue	$285-$332
Ivory	$280-$327
Light Green	$279-$310
Red	$282-$327
Turquoise	$270-$317
Yellow	$260-$310

#6 mixing bowl in red. **$282-$327**

#6 mixing bowl in cobalt blue. **$285-$332**

Photo courtesy Strawser Auctions

#6 mixing bowl in light green. Sold at auction in October 2006 for **$225**.

Mixing bowl #7

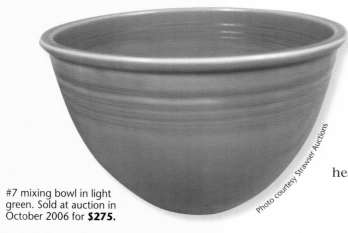

Late in 1942 this size was available only in cobalt blue. Bowls made before 1938 have rings inside the bottom, and are usually marked "Fiesta/HLC USA" with the size number. Bowls made later have no rings and are usually marked with "Fiesta/Made in USA" with the size number. There are no known lids for this size bowl.

The #7 mixing bowl holds the distinction of being the heaviest (6-1/2 pounds) item in the entire Fiesta line.

Photo courtesy Strawser Auctions

#7 mixing bowl in light green. Sold at auction in October 2006 for **$275.**

DEGREE OF DIFFICULTY

3-4

DIMENSIONS:

7-1/8" by 11"

PRODUCTION DATES:

1936 to 1944

COLORS

Cobalt Blue	$549-$599
Ivory	$495-$549
Light Green	$449-$589
Red	$549-$625
Turquoise	$529-$620
Yellow	$449-$589

#7 mixing bowl in ivory. **$495-$549**

#7 mixing bowl in cobalt blue. **$549-$599**

#7 mixing bowl in yellow. **$449-$589**

VINTAGE FIESTA PIECES

fiesta Mixing bowl lids

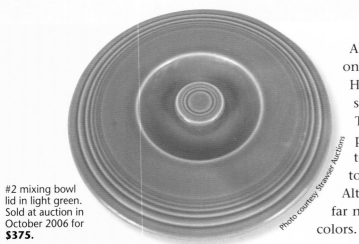

#2 mixing bowl lid in light green. Sold at auction in October 2006 for **$375.**

Photo courtesy Strawser Auctions

Although lids for all seven mixing bowls were modeled, only the four smallest ones were ever put into production. Having been produced for less than half a year, lids are some of the hardest-to-find items in the regular Fiesta line. This may be because so few lids were made (production problems or slow sellers perhaps?) or because it is difficult to pick up the lid by the knob. If you ever have the chance to purchase a #5 or #6 lid, expect to pay $10,000 or more. Although there are rumors of a #7 lid having survived, so far none has surfaced. Lids have been found in the first five colors. No turquoise lid has ever been found.

DEGREE OF DIFFICULTY

5

DIMENSIONS:

#1, 5"; #2, 6"; #3, 6-3/4"; #4, 7-3/4"

PRODUCTION DATES:

for approximately six months in late 1936.

COLORS

Cobalt Blue	$900-$1,100
Ivory	$875-$1,000
Light Green	$800-$900
Red	$900-$1,100
Yellow	$800-$900

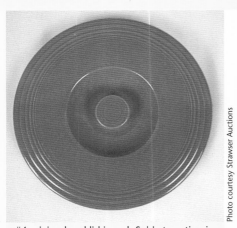

#4 mixing bowl lid in red. Sold at auction in October 2006 for **$350.**

Photo courtesy Strawser Auctions

#4 mixing bowl lid in cobalt blue. Sold at auction in October 2006 for **$275.**

Photo courtesy Strawser Auctions

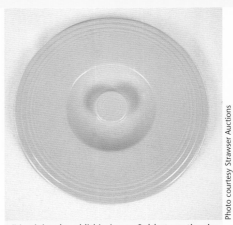

#4 mixing bowl lid in ivory. Sold at auction in October 2006 for **$250.**

Photo courtesy Strawser Auctions

VINTAGE FIESTA PIECES

#4 mixing bowl lid in light green. Sold at auction in October 2006 for **$325.**

#4 mixing bowl lid in yellow. Sold at auction in October 2006 for **$275.**

#3 mixing bowl lid in red. Sold at auction in October 2006 for **$375.**

#3 mixing bowl lid in cobalt blue. Sold at auction in October 2006 for **$350.**

#3 mixing bowl lid in light green. Sold at auction in October 2006 for **$325.**

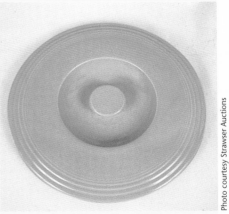

#3 mixing bowl lid in yellow. Sold at auction in October 2006 for **$300.**

#2 mixing bowl lid in red. Sold at auction in October 2006 for **$275.**

#2 mixing bowl lid in cobalt blue. Sold at auction in October 2006 for **$375.**

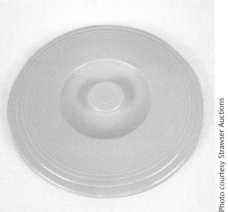

#2 mixing bowl lid in ivory. Sold at auction in October 2006 for **$325.**

VINTAGE FIESTA PIECES

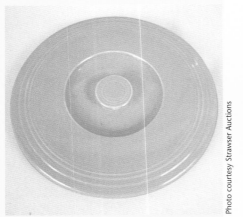

#2 mixing bowl lid in yellow. Sold at auction in October 2006 for **$250.**

Photo courtesy Strawser Auctions

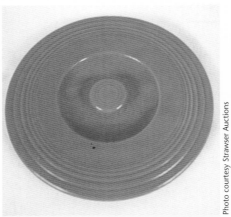

#1 mixing bowl lid in red. Sold at auction in October 2006 for **$325.**

Photo courtesy Strawser Auctions

#1 mixing bowl lid in light green. Sold at auction in October 2006 for **$300.**

Photo courtesy Strawser Auctions

#1 mixing bowl lid in light green, **$800-$900,** and a #4 mixing bowl lid in red, **$900-$1,100.**

Very rare bowl lids in red, **$900-$1,100,** light green, **$800-$900,** and yellow, **$800-$900.**

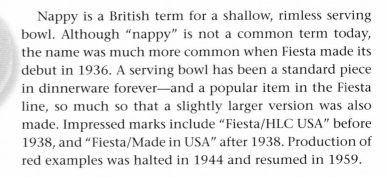

fiesta 8-1/2" Nappy

Nappy is a British term for a shallow, rimless serving bowl. Although "nappy" is not a common term today, the name was much more common when Fiesta made its debut in 1936. A serving bowl has been a standard piece in dinnerware forever—and a popular item in the Fiesta line, so much so that a slightly larger version was also made. Impressed marks include "Fiesta/HLC USA" before 1938, and "Fiesta/Made in USA" after 1938. Production of red examples was halted in 1944 and resumed in 1959.

DEGREE OF DIFFICULTY

1 for the original six colors, 2 for colors of the 1950s, and 3 for medium green.

DIMENSIONS:

8-1/2" by 2-7/8"

PRODUCTION DATES:

1936 to 1969

ORIGINAL COLORS		1950S COLORS	
Cobalt Blue	$53-$58	Chartreuse	$65-$67
Ivory	$50-$57	Forest Green	$60-$63
Light Green	$44-$47	Gray	$59-$61
Red	$55-$60	Rose	$59-$62
Turquoise	$45-$46		
Yellow	$45-$49	Medium Green	$170-$185

8-1/2" nappy in medium green. **$170-$185**

8-1/2" nappy in light green. **$44-$47**

8-1/2" nappy in gray. Sold at auction in October 2006 for **$10.**

Photo courtesy Strawser Auctions

8-1/2" nappy in ivory, with faint spots of sooty discoloration around the rim typical of pieces in this color. **$50-$57**

8-1/2" nappy in rose. **$59-$62**

8-1/2" nappy in chartreuse. **$65-$67**

8-1/2" nappy in yellow. **$45-$49**

8-1/2" nappy in red. **$55-$60**

8-1/2" nappy in turquoise. **$45-$46**

8-1/2" nappy in cobalt blue. **$53-$58**

9-1/2" Nappy

9-1/2" nappy in turquoise. Sold at auction in October 2006 for **$30.**

Photo courtesy Strawser Auctions

Although the 9-1/2" nappy was produced for only 11 years (one-third the length of time the 8-1/2" nappy was produced), examples are still relatively easy to find. Prices for this piece are reasonable and not much more than its sibling, the 8-1/2" nappy. Impressed marks include "Fiesta/HLC USA" (two sizes) before 1938, and "Fiesta/Made in USA" after 1938. Production of red examples was halted in 1944.

DEGREE OF DIFFICULTY

1-2

DIMENSIONS:

9-1/2" by 3-1/8"

PRODUCTION DATES:

1936 to 1947

COLORS

Cobalt Blue	**$70-$75**
Ivory	**$69-$71**
Light Green	**$55-$59**
Red	**$75-$81**
Turquoise	**$56-$59**
Yellow	**$57-$60**

9-1/2" nappy in ivory. **$69-$71**

9-1/2" nappy in red. **$75-$81**

9-1/2" nappy in light green. Sold at auction in October 2006 for **$15.**

Photo courtesy Strawser Auctions

VINTAGE FIESTA PIECES

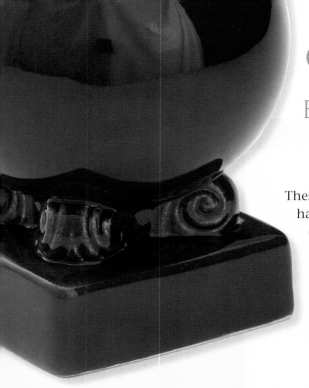

Candleholders
Bulb candleholders

These candleholders are pure art deco. Homemakers of the 1930s must have preferred the bulb candleholders to the tripod variety, as more of them seem to have been purchased. This is a great example of how the Fiesta line was promoted as not only suitable for breakfast and lunch, but for dinner and parties, too. By offering the customer a choice in styles—the plainer bulb style or the more glamorous tripod variety—a sophisticated table could be set. They are marked inside the base "Fiesta HLCo USA." Production of red was halted in 1944.

DEGREE OF DIFFICULTY

2

DIMENSIONS:

3-3/4" by 2-1/2"

PRODUCTION DATES:

1936 to 1946

COLORS

Cobalt Blue	$115-$125/pair
Ivory	$115-$125/pair
Light Green	$95-$115/pair
Red	$120-$130/pair
Turquoise	$115-$125/pair
Yellow	$105-$130/pair

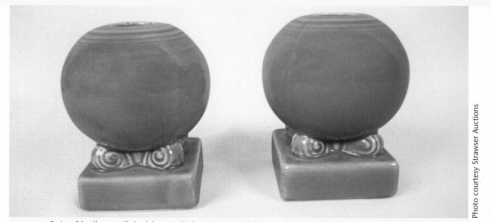

Pair of bulb candleholders in light green. Sold at auction in October 2006 for **$100.**

Photo courtesy Strawser Auctions

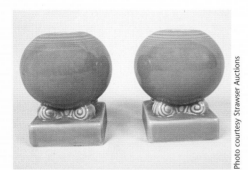

Pair of bulb candleholders in turquoise. Sold at auction in October 2006 for **$85.**

Bulb candleholder in ivory. **$115-$125/pair**

Bulb candleholder in cobalt blue. **$115-$125/pair**

Bulb candleholder in yellow. **$105-$130/pair**

fiesta Tripod candleholders

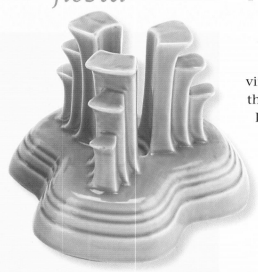

The tripod candleholders are one of the most sought-after items in the vintage Fiesta line. Because they were in production four years less then the bulb candleholder, there are not as many of these on the market. If you are lucky enough to find a pair, check the three "supports" for chips and flaking. They are also part of the post-'86 wares. The early versions are marked with an impressed "Fiesta/HLC USA." One way to tell a vintage holder from a new one (other than by color) is that almost all early holders have a completely glazed base, called a "wet foot." Almost all new holders have the glaze wiped from the base.

DEGREE OF DIFFICULTY

4

DIMENSIONS:

3-1/2" by 4-1/2"

PRODUCTION DATES:

1936 to 1943

ORIGINAL COLORS

Cobalt Blue	$575-$630/pair
Ivory	$600-$650/pair
Light Green	$500-$550/pair
Red	$635-$699/pair
Turquoise	$625-$685/pair
Yellow	$479-$499/pair

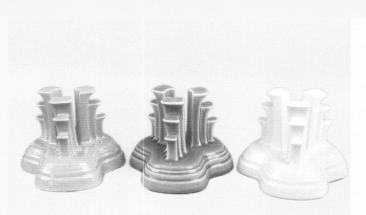

Tripod candleholders in yellow, **$479-$499/pair,** light green, **$500-$550/pair,** and ivory, **$600-$650/pair.**

Tripod candleholders in cobalt blue, **$575-$630/pair,** and red, **$635-$699/pair.**

Tripod candleholders are one of the most sought-after items in the vintage Fiesta line.

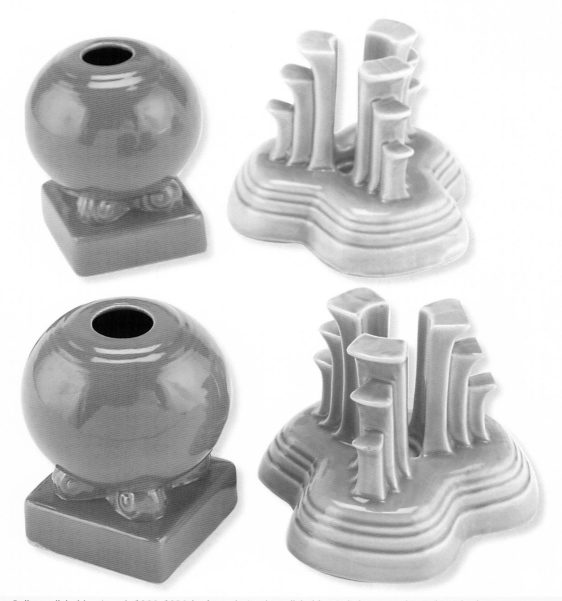

Bulb candleholders in red, **$120-$130/pair**, and tripod candleholders in light green, **$500-$550/pair.**

Carafes

Along with the disk pitcher, the carafe is one of the most photographed pieces of the entire Fiesta line—perhaps because its style represents art deco in its purist form. The stopper has a cork attached. Before buying, check the cork and the area around the cork for deterioration and damage. This part of the stopper is prone to chipping and cracking. The carafe holds 6-1/2 cups. It is marked with an impressed "Fiesta/HLC USA." Ivory is the hardest color to find, followed closely by red. Production of red was halted in 1944.

DEGREE OF DIFFICULTY

2-3

DIMENSIONS:

9-1/4" by 7-1/8" by 6-1/8"

PRODUCTION DATES:

1936 to 1947

COLORS

Cobalt Blue	$300-$345
Ivory	$310-$320
Light Green	$275-$295
Red	$295-$335
Turquoise	$265-$300
Yellow	$250-$285

Carafe in red. **$295-$335**

Carafe in turquoise. **$265-$300**

Carafe in yellow. **$250-$285**

Carafe in cobalt blue. **$300-$345**

Carafes in red, **$295-$335,** and ivory, **$310-$320.**

Carafe in light green. **$275-$295**

VINTAGE FIESTA PIECES

Casseroles

Covered casserole

In terms of styling, the covered casserole is a larger version of the covered onion soup bowl and a shirt-tale relative of the sugar bowl. A covered dish has been a standard piece in almost all dinnerware sets, regardless of the country of origin. Although covered casseroles were made for 33 years, examples in good condition are not as easy to find as you would think. Because the handles were applied by hand, you may find some that are crooked or not directly across from each other. The casserole has two impressed marks: "Fiesta/HLC USA" and the later "Fiesta/Made in USA." Production of red examples was halted in 1944 and resumed in 1959.

DEGREE OF DIFFICULTY

2 for the original colors;
3 for the colors of the 1950s and medium green.

DIMENSIONS:

9-3/4" by 7-7/8" by 5-3/4" tall with lid

PRODUCTION DATES:

1936 to 1969

ORIGINAL COLORS		1950S COLORS	
Cobalt Blue	$195-$215	Chartreuse	$250-$260
Ivory	$225-$249	Forest Green	$285-$300
Light Green	$140-$160	Gray	$255-$270
Red	$235-$279	Rose	$285-$300
Turquoise	$150-$160		
Yellow	$145-$160	Medium Green	$1,385-$1,495

Covered casserole in red, **$235-$279**, and yellow, **$145-$160**.

Covered casserole in forest green. Sold at auction in October 2006 for **$130.**

Photo courtesy Strawser Auctions

Covered casserole in chartreuse. Sold at auction in October 2006 for **$140.**

Photo courtesy Strawser Auctions

Covered casserole in cobalt blue. Sold at auction in October 2006 for **$50.**

Photo courtesy Strawser Auctions

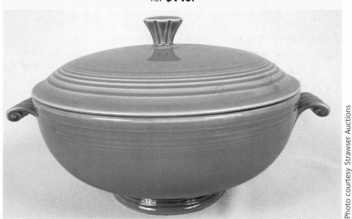

Covered casserole in turquoise. Sold at auction in October 2006 for **$70.**

Photo courtesy Strawser Auctions

Covered casserole in medium green. Sold at auction in October 2006 for **$425.**

Photo courtesy Strawser Auctions

Covered casserole in light green. Sold at auction in October 2006 for **$50.**

Photo courtesy Strawser Auctions

VINTAGE FIESTA PIECES

Covered casserole

Covered casserole in rose. **$285-$300**

Covered casserole in yellow. **$145-$160**

Covered casserole in red. **$235-$279**

Covered casserole in red, **$235-$279**, and yellow, **$145-$160**.

Coffeepots

Coffeepot

The coffeepot seems to have sold well in the early years of Fiesta, judging from the number that have survived. The same cannot be said for coffeepots in the colors of the 1950s. Forest green, chartreuse, and rose are all hard to find, but it is the last color of the 1950s, gray, that tops the list. The coffeepot is the second tallest piece (just 1-3/4" smaller than the 12" vase) in the Fiesta line. It holds seven cups and can be marked "Fiesta/HLC USA" or "Fiesta/Made in USA." Examples in gray bring a premium. Production of red was halted in 1944.

DEGREE OF DIFFICULTY

2-3

DIMENSIONS:

10-1/2" by 8" by 4-1/2" (lid)

PRODUCTION DATES:

1936 to 1959

ORIGINAL COLORS		1950S COLORS	
Cobalt Blue	$238-$270	Chartreuse	$410-$460
Ivory	$230-$255	Forest Green	$458-$495
Light Green	$195-$220	Gray	$625-$665
Red	$250-$275	Rose	$475-$520
Turquoise	$185-$210		
Yellow	$185-$218		

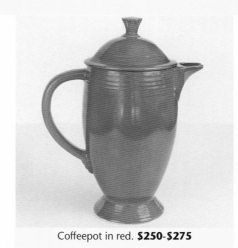

Coffeepot in red. **$250-$275**

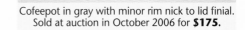

Cofeepot in gray with minor rim nick to lid finial. Sold at auction in October 2006 for **$175.**

Photo courtesy Strawser Auctions

Coffeepot in chartreuse. Sold at auction in October 2006 for **$200.**

Photo courtesy Strawser Auctions

Coffeepot in rose. Sold at auction in October 2006 for **$165.**

Photo courtesy Strawser Auctions

Coffeepot in turquoise. Sold at auction in October 2006 for **$100.**

Photo courtesy Strawser Auctions

Coffeepot in light green. Sold at auction in October 2006 for **$115.**

Photo courtesy Strawser Auctions

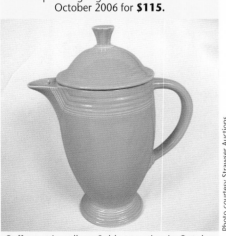

Coffeepot in yellow. Sold at auction in October 2006 for **$135.**

Photo courtesy Strawser Auctions

Coffeepot in cobalt blue. **$238-$270**

fiesta Demitasse coffeepot

Also called "After Dinner" or "A.D.," this coffeepot was designed to be used for an after dinner beverage (Turkish coffee, demitasse, or even hot chocolate). With the exception of the handle, this piece is a scaled-down version of the coffeepot. The vent hole in the cover was put in by hand, so you may find a cover without the hole added. Sometimes the vent hole is in a different part of the cover. The demitasse coffeepot is marked "Fiesta/HLC USA."

DEGREE OF DIFFICULTY

3-4

DIMENSIONS:

7-1/2" by 7" by 3-1/2" (lid)

PRODUCTION DATES:

1936 to 1943

COLORS

Cobalt Blue	**$490-$520**
Ivory	**$510-$550**
Light Green	**$475-$525**
Red	**$595-$650**
Turquoise	**$650-$695**
Yellow	**$450-$500**

Demitasse coffeepot in light green.
$475-$525

Demitasse coffeepot in turquoise, **$650-$695,** and red, **$595-$650.**

Demitasse coffeepot in yellow. **$450-$500**

Demitasse coffeepot in cobalt blue. Sold at auction in October 2006 for **$300.**

Photo courtesy Strawser Auctions

Demitasse coffeepot and cups and saucers in original colors.

Comports

Comport (called the 12" comport)

A multi-purpose item, this piece could be used as a centerpiece bowl on a table, along with a pair of candleholders, or as a salad bowl. The foot was made separately and then applied by hand, so examine the bottom of the piece before you buy. You may notice the base just off slightly so that the bowl does not sit straight. The foot adds elegance to an otherwise utilitarian bowl. These comports may be found unmarked or with a "Genuine Fiesta" stamp. Production of red was halted in 1944.

DEGREE OF DIFFICULTY

3

DIMENSIONS:

12-1/2" by 3-1/2

PRODUCTION DATES:

1936 to 1946

COLORS

Cobalt Blue	$175-$195
Ivory	$170-$190
Light Green	$150-$165
Red	$190-$200
Turquoise	$160-$175
Yellow	$175-$180

Comport in turquoise. Sold at auction in October 2006 for **$80.**

Photo courtesy Strawser Auctions

Comport in ivory. **$170-$190**

Photo courtesy Strawser Auctions

Comport in light green with rim glaze imperfection. Sold at auction in October 2006 for **$45.**

Comport in cobalt blue. **$175-$195**

Comport in red. **$190-$200**

fiesta   Sweets comport

Sweets comport in cobalt blue. **$85-$95**

The addition of the tall foot adds to the charm of this piece, which works well for holding candy or nuts. Sweets comports seemed to have sold well during their 11 years of production as they can be found without too much trouble. Again, like the comport, the two pieces of the sweets comports were put together with liquid clay (slip) and then fired. Examine the piece before you buy it to make sure the top is straight. Sweets comports may be found with an "HLCo USA" stamp, but they are seldom marked. Production of red was halted in 1944.

DEGREE OF DIFFICULTY

2

DIMENSIONS:

5-1/8" by 3-1/2"

PRODUCTION DATES:

1936 to 1947

COLORS

Cobalt Blue	**$85-$95**
Ivory	**$80-$95**
Light Green	**$80-$85**
Red	**$100-$115**
Turquoise	**$80-$90**
Yellow	**$70-$79**

Sweets comport in red. Sold at auction in October 2006 for **$105**.

Sweets comport in ivory, ink stamped HLC USA. Sold at auction in October 2006 for **$105**.

Photo courtesy Strawser Auctions

Photo courtesy Strawser Auctions

Sweets comports in yellow, **$70-$79,** and light green, **$80-$85.**

Sweets comport in cobalt blue, **$85-$95,** with sauceboat in light green.

Creamers & Sugar Bowls
Ring-handle creamer

The ring-handle creamer replaced the stick-handle creamer in late 1938. The body is the same as the stick-handle creamer, but the handle portion is different. The stick-handle creamer, which had a handle like that on the demitasse coffeepot, was restyled into the ring-handle model, which matched the teacup and other ring-handled items in the line. With the handle opposite the spout, the ring-handle creamer was easy for left-handed people to use.

Production of red examples was halted in 1944 and resumed in 1959.

DEGREE OF DIFFICULTY

1

DIMENSIONS:
5-7/8" by 3" by 3-5/8"

PRODUCTION DATES:
1938 to 1969

ORIGINAL COLORS		1950S COLORS	
Cobalt Blue	$32-$39	Chartreuse	$42-$46
Ivory	$32-$38	Forest Green	$40-$44
Light Green	$26-$29	Gray	$40-$50
Red	$36-$41	Rose	$40-$50
Turquoise	$23-$28		
Yellow	$26-$29	Medium Green	$120-$135

Ring-handle creamer and covered sugar bowl in medium green. **$120-$135** for the creamer and **$195-$215** for the sugar bowl.

Photo courtesy Strawser Auctions

Ring-handle creamer and covered sugar bowl in chartreuse. Sold at auction in October 2006 for **$50.**

Photo courtesy Strawser Auctions

Ring-handle creamer and covered sugar bowl in cobalt blue. Sold at auction in October 2006 for **$45.**

Photo courtesy Strawser Auctions

Ring-handle creamer and covered sugar bowl in ivory. Sold at auction in October 2006 for **$50.**

VINTAGE FIESTA PIECES

Ring-handle creamer

Ring-handle creamer and covered sugar bowl in turquoise. Sold at auction in October 2006 for **$35.**

Ring-handle creamer and covered sugar bowl in yellow. Sold at auction in October 2006 for **$25.**

Ring-handle creamer and covered sugar bowl in forest green. Sold at auction in October 2006 for **$80.**

Ring-handle creamer in rose. **$40-$50**

Photo courtesy Strawser Auctions

Creamer in medium green, in original box. Sold at auction in October 2006 for **$95.**

Ring-handle creamer in turquoise. **$23-$28**

fiesta Stick-handle creamer

Produced for less than three years, this creamer was one of the first Fiesta items to be restyled. Because of the late introduction of turquoise in mid-1937, this piece is slightly harder to find in that color. The creamer is easy for right-handed people to use, but is difficult for left-handed people to use. The stick-handle creamer, which matched the after-dinner—or demitasse—coffeepot, was succeeded by the more versatile ring-handle creamer. It bears an impressed "HLC USA" mark.

DEGREE OF DIFFICULTY

2-3

DIMENSIONS:

4-5/8" by 3" by 3-5/8" without handle

PRODUCTION DATES:

1936 to 1938

COLORS

Cobalt Blue	$60-$68
Ivory	$62-$68
Light Green	$45-$49
Red	$65-$72
Turquoise	$85-$95
Yellow	$45-$49

Stick-handle creamer in yellow. **$45-$49**

Stick-handle creamer in cobalt blue with minor rim nick. Sold at auction in October 2006 for **$10**.

Photo courtesy Strawser Auctions

Stick-handle creamer in ivory. **$62-$68**

VINTAGE FIESTA PIECES

Photo courtesy Strawser Auctions

Stick-handle creamer in red. Sold at auction in October 2006 for **$45.**

The stick-handle creamer "is difficult for left-handed people to use."

Photo courtesy Strawser Auctions

Stick-handle creamer in light green. Sold at auction in October 2006 for **$25.**

fiesta

Sugar Bowl

Also called the covered sugar

A standard item in dinnerware sets, the sugar bowl enjoyed a 33-year run. It underwent an early design change just months after introduction. Check the inside bottom of the sugar bowl. Sugar bowls with flat bottoms are hard to find as they were only made at the beginning of 1936. After a few months, the inside of the sugar bowl was rounded. Also check the handles on your sugar bowl. Because they were applied by hand, like the handles on the casserole, they may be crooked or not directly across from each other. The sugar bowl can be marked either "Fiesta/HLC U.S.A." or "Made in U.S.A." Those in 1950s colors may have a foot that is slightly less flared. Production of red examples was halted in 1944 and resumed in 1959.

Covered sugar in turquoise.
$49-$58

DEGREE OF DIFFICULTY

1-2 for all colors except medium green, which ranks 2-3.

DIMENSIONS:

3-3/4" without handles by 5" with cover

PRODUCTION DATES:

1936 to 1969

ORIGINAL COLORS		1950S COLORS	
Cobalt Blue	$58-$70	Chartreuse	$69-$77
Ivory	$58-$70	Forest Green	$72-$78
Light Green	$48-$55	Gray	$68-$75
Red	$60-$72	Rose	$70-$78
Turquoise	$49-$58		
Yellow	$48-$57	Medium Green	$195-$215

Covered sugar bowl, **$60-$72**, and stick-handle creamer in red, **$65-$72**.

Covered sugar bowl in yellow, **$48-$57,** ring-handle creamer in light green, **$26-$29**, and stick handle creamer in red, **$65-$72.**

Cups & Mugs

Demitasse cup and saucer

Also called "After Dinner" or "A.D."

Designed to go along with the after dinner or demitasse coffeepot, this cup looks like a scaled-down version of a teacup or eggcup with a stick handle. Before Starbucks, after dinner demitasse or Turkish coffee was the rage in the late 1930s and early 1940s. Demitasse cups are rarely marked, and they also vary in style details: Cups made before late 1937 have a flat inner bottom; those made after that time have a rounded inner bottom. Early demitasse saucers also have two rings around the base or foot; examples after 1937 have a single ring and are usually stamped "Genuine Fiesta." Because the handles were applied by hand, they may not be perfectly straight. Production of red examples was halted in 1944.

DEGREE OF DIFFICULTY

2-3 for the original six colors, 3-4 for colors of the 1950s.

DIMENSIONS:

Cup, 2-1/2" by 2-1/2" without handle by 2-1/2", and saucer, 5-1/4" diameter by 3/4"

PRODUCTION DATES:

1936 to 1959

ORIGINAL COLORS		1950S COLORS	
Cobalt Blue	$80-$92/set	Chartreuse	$495-$520/set
Ivory	$80-$90/set	Forest Green	$490-$520/set
Light Green	$78-$80/set	Gray	$495-$535/set
Red	$90-$105/set	Rose	$490-$515/set
Turquoise	$80-$85/set		
Yellow	$60-$79/set		

Demitasse cup and saucer in cobalt blue. **$80-$92/set**

Demitasse cups and saucers in ivory, **$80-$90/set,** and red, **$90-$105/set.**

Demitasse cup and saucer in turquoise. Sold at auction in October 2006 for **$40.**

Rare demitasse cup and saucer in forest green. Sold at auction in October 2006 for **$200.**

Demitasse cup and saucer in light green. **$78-$80/set**

Photo courtesy Strawser Auctions

Rare demitasse cup and saucer in chartreuse. Sold at auction in October 2006 for **$200.**

Photo courtesy Strawser Auctions

Rare demitasse cup and saucer in gray. Sold at auction in October 2006 for **$225.**

Photo courtesy Strawser Auctions

Demitasse cup and saucer in yellow. **$60-$79/set**

VINTAGE FIESTA PIECES

fiesta Eggcup

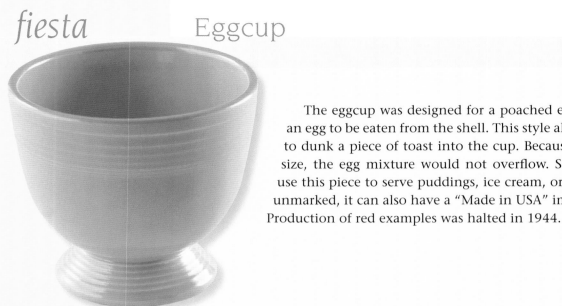

The eggcup was designed for a poached egg rather than an egg to be eaten from the shell. This style allowed the user to dunk a piece of toast into the cup. Because of the larger size, the egg mixture would not overflow. Some collectors use this piece to serve puddings, ice cream, or gelatin. Often unmarked, it can also have a "Made in USA" impressed mark. Production of red examples was halted in 1944.

DEGREE OF DIFFICULTY

2-3 for the six original colors, 3-4 for colors of the 1950s.

DIMENSIONS:

3-3/8" by 3-1/8"

PRODUCTION DATES:

1936 to 1959

ORIGINAL COLORS

Cobalt Blue	$68-$76
Ivory	$66-$72
Light Green	$55-$66
Red	$70-$85
Turquoise	$56-$65
Yellow	$56-$64

1950S COLORS

Chartreuse	$148-$160
Forest Green	$150-$165
Gray	$160-$165
Rose	$150-$165

Eggcup in yellow. **$56-$64**

Eggcup in forest green. Sold at auction in October 2006 for **$25**.

Photo courtesy Strawser Auctions

Eggcup in chartreuse. Sold at auction in October 2006 for **$45**.

Photo courtesy Strawser Auctions

VINTAGE FIESTA PIECES

Eggcup in gray. Sold at auction in October 2006 for **$65.**

Photo courtesy Strawser Auctions

Eggcup in rose. Sold at auction in October 2006 for **$55.**

Photo courtesy Strawser Auctions

Eggcup in turquoise. **$56-$65**

Some collectors use the eggcup to serve puddings, ice cream, or gelatin.

Eggcup in red. **$70-$85**

Eggcup in light green. **$55-$66**

Eggcup in ivory. **$66-$72**

Eggcup in yellow, **$56-$64,** with light green ashtray, **$49-$54.**

Teacup and saucer

Teacup and saucer in ivory.
$35-$43/set

In the product line for more than 33 years, the teacup and saucer are not hard to find. No doubt they were good sellers. The teacup and saucer come in three variations. Cups made up to 1937 have a flat inner bottom and rings inside the rim; saucers have five rings around the base or foot; neither is marked. Cups made after 1937 have a rounded inner bottom, inner rim rings, and are rarely marked, while the saucers have a single wide ring under the rim and a "Genuine Fiesta" stamp. In the 1960s, the cup was slightly enlarged and redesigned without a turned foot or rings inside the rim; the saucers are slightly deeper with a double band of rings under the rim, and a "Genuine Fiesta" stamp. Production of red examples was halted in 1944 and resumed in 1959.

DEGREE OF DIFFICULTY

1-2 for the six original colors;
2 for the colors of the 1950s; and
2-3 for medium green.

DIMENSIONS:

Cup, 3-1/2" by 2-3/4" without handle, and saucer, 6" diameter by 3/4"

PRODUCTION DATES:

1938 to 1969

ORIGINAL COLORS

Cobalt Blue	$36-$44/set
Ivory	$35-$43/set
Light Green	$29-$34/set
Red	$40-$50/set
Turquoise	$34-$38/set
Yellow	$29-$33/set

1950S COLORS

Chartreuse	$40-$45/set
Forest Green	$44-$49/set
Gray	$36-$43/set
Rose	$42-$51/set
Medium Green	$60-$70/set

Two teacups and saucers in medium green, in original boxes. Sold at auction in October 2006 for **$160.**

Photo courtesy Strawser Auctions

Teacup and saucer group in 1950s colors: medium green, forest green, chartreuse, rose, and gray. Sold at auction in October 2006 for **$70.**

Teacup and saucer in forest green. **$44-$49/set**

Teacup and saucer group in 1950s colors: medium green, forest green, chartreuse, rose, and gray. Sold at auction in October 2006 for **$80.**

Teacup and saucer in medium green. **$60-$70/set**

Teacup and saucer group in six original colors: red, cobalt blue, ivory, light green, yellow, and turquoise. Sold at auction in October 2006 for **$55.**

Teacup and saucer in gray. **$36-$43/set**

Photo courtesy Strawser Auctions

VINTAGE FIESTA PIECES

Teacup and saucer

Teacup and saucer in rose. **$42-$51/set**

Teacup and saucer in yellow. **$29-$33/set**

In the product line for more than 33 years, the teacup and saucer are not hard to find.

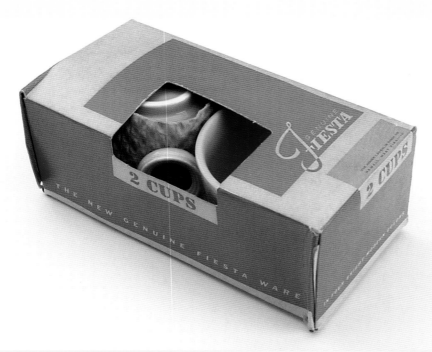

Unopened boxed set of two teacups in yellow. Boxes can double or triple the overall value of the piece.

Teacup and saucer in cobalt blue. **$36-$44/set**

fiesta Tom & Jerry mug

Tom & Jerry mug in medium green.
$125-$140

A Tom & Jerry is a hot alcoholic drink made with eggs, sugar, and whiskey. The Tom & Jerry mug is one of two Fiesta pieces that do not have the familiar band of rings for which Fiesta is famous. (The other item is the syrup pitcher.) Today's collectors use this mug for coffee or tea. You will often find the Tom & Jerry mug in white with "Tom & Jerry" in gold, part of the Tom & Jerry set that also included a footed salad bowl used to hold the beverage. This is another item that varies in terms of thickness. Some mugs are much heavier than others, and the topside walls are thicker than others. When marked, the mugs bear the "Genuine Fiesta" stamp. Production of red examples was halted in 1944 and resumed in 1959.

DEGREE OF DIFFICULTY

2 for all colors except medium green, which is a 3.

DIMENSIONS:

3-1/8" by 4-3/8"

PRODUCTION DATES:

1936 until 1969

ORIGINAL COLORS		1950S COLORS	
Cobalt Blue	$75-$82	Chartreuse	$84-$88
Ivory	$76-$84	Forest Green	$80-$85
Light Green	$65-$69	Gray	$82-$86
Red	$79-$88	Rose	$86-$89
Turquoise	$60-$65		
Yellow	$65-$68	Medium Green	$125-$140

Tom & Jerry mug in rose. Sold at auction in October 2006 for **$15.**

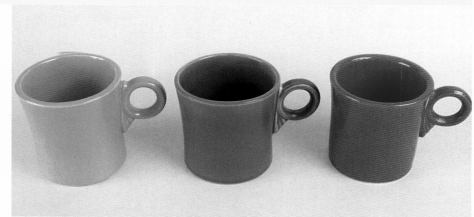

Three Tom & Jerry mugs in yellow, **$65-$68,** light green, **$65-$69,** and red, **$79-$88.**

Tom & Jerry punch bowl with two ring-handled mugs, nine Tom & Jerry mugs, and 11 non-Fiesta Tom & Jerry mugs. Sold at auction in October 2006 for **$35.**

Three Tom & Jerry mugs in forest green, **$80-$85,** gray, **$82-$86,** and chartreuse, **$84-$88.**

Tom & Jerry mugs in the original six colors.

Jars

Marmalade

Red marmalade jars are harder to find than the other colors, probably due to the fact that their production run was three years shorter than the other colors. The slot in the lid, for a spoon, was hand-cut, so slot sizes vary from lid to lid. Marmalade jars are marked on the base "Fiesta/HLC USA." Production of red examples was halted in 1944.

DEGREE OF DIFFICULTY

3-4

DIMENSIONS:

3-1/8" by 4-1/16" with lid

PRODUCTION DATES:

1936 to 1946

COLORS

Cobalt Blue	$345-$385
Ivory	$350-$370
Light Green	$325-$375
Red	$365-$410
Turquoise	$360-$395
Yellow	$315-$355

Photo courtesy Strawser Auctions

Marmalades in red, **$365-$410**, and ivory, **$350-$370**, including glass spoons with colored tips.

Marmalade jar in light green with metal holder. Sold at auction in October 2006 for **$275**.

Marmalade jar in yellow. Sold at auction in October 2006 for **$185.**

Marmalade jar in cobalt blue. Sold at auction in October 2006 for **$190.**

Marmalade jar in ivory. **$350-$370**

Marmalade jar in light green. **$325-$375**

VINTAGE FIESTA PIECES

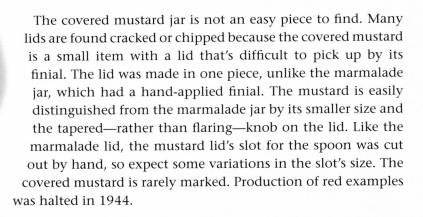

fiesta Mustard

The covered mustard jar is not an easy piece to find. Many lids are found cracked or chipped because the covered mustard is a small item with a lid that's difficult to pick up by its finial. The lid was made in one piece, unlike the marmalade jar, which had a hand-applied finial. The mustard is easily distinguished from the marmalade jar by its smaller size and the tapered—rather than flaring—knob on the lid. Like the marmalade lid, the mustard lid's slot for the spoon was cut out by hand, so expect some variations in the slot's size. The covered mustard is rarely marked. Production of red examples was halted in 1944.

DEGREE OF DIFFICULTY

3-4

DIMENSIONS:

2-1/2" by 3-1/16" with lid

PRODUCTION DATES:

1936 to 1946

COLORS

Cobalt Blue	**$352-$340**
Ivory	**$335-$350**
Light Green	**$260-$280**
Red	**$330-$350**
Turquoise	**$295-$320**
Yellow	**$270-$295**

Two mustards in red, **$330-$350**, and ivory, **$335-$350**.

Three mustards in yellow, **$270-$295,** light green, **$260-$280,** and turquoise, **$295-$320.**

The mustard is easily distinguished from the marmalade jar by its smaller size and the tapered—rather than flaring—knob on the lid.

Covered mustard in ivory, **$335-$350,** with marmalade jar in light green, **$325-$375.**

Pitchers and Jugs

Disk water pitcher

If there is one piece of Fiesta that sums up the feel of the line, it is the disk water pitcher. Flat, yet three-dimensional, this piece is a striking addition to any table. It is also used in advertisements for other products. Recently a greeting card company used a yellow disk water pitcher, filled with flowers, on a get-well card.

With a capacity of 70 ounces, the disk water pitcher was in production for almost 31 years. It is also part of the post-1986 line in contemporary colors. Pitchers produced by other manufacturers in this same shape are common, so look for the "Fiesta/Made in USA" impressed mark. Production of red examples was halted in 1944 and resumed in 1959.

DEGREE OF DIFFICULTY

1-2 for the six original colors, 3-4 for colors of the 1950s, and 5 for medium green.

DIMENSIONS:

7-1/2" by 8-3/4" by 5"

PRODUCTION DATES:

1938 to 1969

ORIGINAL COLORS		1950S COLORS	
Cobalt Blue	$155-$175	Chartreuse	$235-$260
Ivory	$155-$170	Forest Green	$225-$265
Light Green	$110-$120	Gray	$225-$250
Red	$170-$190	Rose	$245-$285
Turquoise	$115-$125		
Yellow	$115-$125	Medium Green	$1,500-$1,600

Disk water pitcher in cobalt blue. **$155-$175**

Disk water pitcher in light green. **$110-$120**

Disk water pitcher in gray. Sold at auction in October 2006 for **$100.**

Photo courtesy Strawser Auctions

Disk water pitcher in yellow. **$115-$125**

Disk water pitcher in ivory. **$155-$170**

Disk water pitcher in red. **$170-$190**

Disk water pitcher in medium green. **$1,500-$1,600**

VINTAGE FIESTA PIECES

Disk water pitcher

Disk water pitcher in forest green. Sold at auction in October 2006 for **$180.**

Photo courtesy Strawser Auctions

Disk water pitcher in chartreuse. Sold at auction in October 2006 for **$100.**

Photo courtesy Strawser Auctions

Disk water pitcher in turquoise. **$115-$125**

Disk water pitcher in rose. **$245-$285**

fiesta Ice pitcher

Ice pitcher in light green. **$140-$150**

Many a novice collector has mistaken the ice pitcher for one of Fiesta's two teapots. If you look closely, the ice pitcher resembles the bottom of a large teapot, but with a medium teapot handle. Its design may suggest otherwise, but it does not have a lid. Even though this piece was in production for more than 10 years, it is not easy to find. This may be due to the fact that the disk water pitcher was more popular with buyers. Often incorrectly called the "ice lip" pitcher, it is marked "HLC USA." The ice pitcher has a capacity of 65 ounces. Production of red examples was halted in 1944.

DEGREE OF DIFFICULTY

2 -3

DIMENSIONS:

6-1/2" by 9-3/4" by 6-1/2"

PRODUCTION DATES:

1936 to 1946

COLORS

Cobalt Blue	$140-$155
Light Green	$140-$150
Ivory	$140-$160
Red	$145-$170
Turquoise	$145-$165
Yellow	$135-$145

Photo courtesy Strawser Auctions

Ice pitcher in cobalt blue. Sold at auction in October 2006 for **$35.**

Two-pint jug in light green, **$90-$95**, with ice pitcher in ivory, **$140-$160.**

Ice pitcher in ivory. **$140-$160**

Ice pitcher in turquoise. Sold at auction in October 2006 for **$55.**

Photo courtesy Strawser Auctions

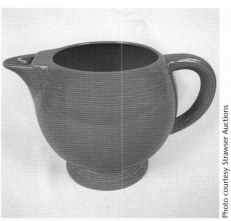

Ice pitcher in red. Sold at auction in October 2006 for **$70.**

Photo courtesy Strawser Auctions

Ice pitcher in yellow. **$135-$145**

Syrup pitcher with "DripCut" top

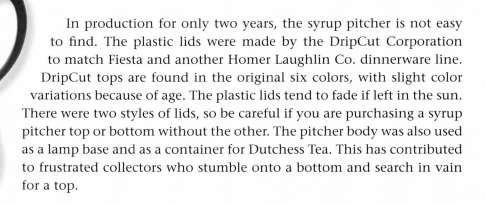

DripCut syrup pitcher in cobalt blue with a blue top, marked Fiesta. **$420-$440**

In production for only two years, the syrup pitcher is not easy to find. The plastic lids were made by the DripCut Corporation to match Fiesta and another Homer Laughlin Co. dinnerware line. DripCut tops are found in the original six colors, with slight color variations because of age. The plastic lids tend to fade if left in the sun. There were two styles of lids, so be careful if you are purchasing a syrup pitcher top or bottom without the other. The pitcher body was also used as a lamp base and as a container for Dutchess Tea. This has contributed to frustrated collectors who stumble onto a bottom and search in vain for a top.

DEGREE OF DIFFICULTY

3-4

DIMENSIONS:

5-3/4", including top, by 3-5/8" without handle

PRODUCTION DATES:

1938 to 1940

COLORS

Cobalt Blue	**$420-$440**
Ivory	**$420-$440**
Light Green	**$350-$365**
Red	**$425-$450**
Turquoise	**$400-$430**
Yellow	**$350-$365**

Syrup pitcher in light green. Sold at auction in October 2006 for **$180**.

Photo courtesy Strawser Auctions

Syrup pitcher in yellow. Sold at auction in October 2006 for **$200**.

Photo courtesy Strawser Auctions

DripCut syrup pitcher in red. Sold at auction in October 2006 for **$200**.

Photo courtesy Strawser Auctions

Syrup pitcher in turquoise. Sold at auction in October 2006 for **$200**.

Photo courtesy Strawser Auctions

DripCut syrup pitcher in ivory. **$420-$440**

fiesta Two-pint jug

Two-pint jug in turquoise. **$90-$95**

The two-pint jug was originally planned to be part of a five-piece set of jugs, with sizes ranging from one-half cup to two pints. The idea of having a service of different-sized jugs for various kitchen tasks was not novel, as other potteries had them before the advent of Fiesta. The two-pint jug was the only size produced. It may be marked "HLC USA" with a "5" near the Fiesta logo, or "Made in USA" without the number. Production of red examples was halted in 1944.

DEGREE OF DIFFICULTY

2-3 (There is not much difference in the degree of difficulty between the six original colors and the colors of the 1950s.)

DIMENSIONS:

4-1/4" by 8-1/2" by 5-1/2"

PRODUCTION DATES:

1936 to 1959

ORIGINAL COLORS

Cobalt Blue	$110-$125
Ivory	$110-$115
Light Green	$90-$95
Red	$115-$135
Turquoise	$90-$95
Yellow	$85-$90

1950S COLORS

Chartreuse	$130-$140
Forest Green	$135-$140
Gray	$155-$160
Rose	$150-$160

Two-pint jug in forest green. Sold at auction in October 2006 for **$70.**

Photo courtesy Strawser Auctions

Two-pint jug in cobalt blue. Sold at auction in October 2006 for **$55.**

Photo courtesy Strawser Auctions

Two-pint jug in yellow. Sold at auction in October 2006 for **$40.**

Photo courtesy Strawser Auctions

VINTAGE FIESTA PIECES

Two-pint jug in chartreuse. **$130-$140**

The two-pint jug was originallly planned to be part of a five-piece set of jugs.

Two-pint jug in rose. **$150-$160**

Two-pint jug in red. **$115-$135**

Two-pint jugs in turquoise, **$90-$95,** and red, **$115-$135.**

Two-pint jug in light green, **$90-$95,** with ice pitcher in ivory, **$140-$160.**

Plates

6" Plate

Also known as a bread and butter plate, the 6" plate was in the line from the time Fiesta appeared on the market until the plate was restyled in 1969. Along with the 7" and 9" plates, the 6" plate is very easy to locate, thus the lower prices. Most 6" plates have a "Genuine Fiesta" stamp. Production of red examples was halted in 1944 and resumed in 1959.

DEGREE OF DIFFICULTY

1

DIMENSIONS:

6-1/2" diameter by 5/8" thick

PRODUCTION DATES:

1936 to 1969

ORIGINAL COLORS		1950S COLORS	
Cobalt Blue	$7-$8	Chartreuse	$9-$11
Ivory	$6-$7	Forest Green	$9-$10
Light Green	$6-$7	Gray	$10-$11
Red	$8-$9	Rose	$9-$11
Turquoise	$6-$7		
Yellow	$6-$7	Medium Green	$21-$28

6" plate in gray. **$10-$11**

Group of 6" plates, one of each in the 11 colors. Sold at auction in October 2006 for **$55**.

Photo courtesy Strawser Auctions

6" and 7" plates in red. **$8-$9** and **$12-$15**, respectively

6" and 7" plates in medium green. **$21-$28** and **$40-$42**, respectively

Group of 6" plates, one of each in the 11 colors. Sold at auction in October 2006 for **$55.**

Photo courtesy Strawser Auctions

VINTAGE FIESTA PIECES

fiesta 7" Plate

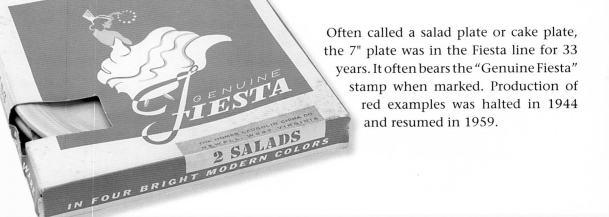

Unopened original box of Fiesta containing two salad plates in yellow. Boxes can double or triple the overall value of the pieces they contain.

Often called a salad plate or cake plate, the 7" plate was in the Fiesta line for 33 years. It often bears the "Genuine Fiesta" stamp when marked. Production of red examples was halted in 1944 and resumed in 1959.

DEGREE OF DIFFICULTY

1

DIMENSIONS:

Actual diameter 7-1/2" by 5/8" thick

PRODUCTION DATES:

1936 to 1969

ORIGINAL COLORS		1950S COLORS	
Cobalt Blue	$10-$12	Chartreuse	$14-$16
Ivory	$10-$12	Forest Green	$15-$17
Light Green	$10-$11	Gray	$15-$17
Red	$12-$15	Rose	$15-$17
Turquoise	$9-$10		
Yellow	$9-$10	Medium Green	$42-$45

Group of 7" plates, one of each in the 11 colors. Sold at auction in October 2006 for **$120.**

Photo courtesy Strawser Auctions

6" and 7" plates in medium green. **$21-$28** and **$42-$45,** respectively.

6" and 7" plates in ivory. **$6-$7** and **$10-$12,** respectively.

Photo courtesy Strawser Auctions

Group of 7" plates, one of each in the 11 colors. Sold at auction in October 2006 for **$105.**

7" plates (top to bottom): yellow, **$9-$10**, turquoise, **$9-$10**, red, **$12-$15**, forest green, **$15-$17**, light green, **$10-$11**, chartreuse, **$14-$16**, cobalt blue, **$10-$12**, rose, **$15-$17**, and ivory, **$10-$12**.

7" plates in light green, cobalt blue, turquoise, yellow, and red.

fiesta 9" Plate

9" plate in yellow. $12-$15

What was the very first item that was modeled for the Fiesta line? If you said the 9" plate, move to the head of the class. Nine-inch plates were often included in boxed sets of Fiesta dishes, perhaps sold as a luncheon set. Because of this, 9" plates are far easier to locate today than the 10" dinner plates. The 9" plate often bears the "Genuine Fiesta" stamp when marked. Note the three sagger pin marks on the bottom of the plates. Production of red examples was halted in 1944 and resumed in 1959.

DEGREE OF DIFFICULTY

1

DIMENSIONS:

Actual diameter 9-1/2" by 3/4" thick

PRODUCTION DATES:

1936 to 1969

ORIGINAL COLORS

Cobalt Blue	$17-$19
Ivory	$17-$18
Light Green	$12-$15
Red	$18-$20
Turquoise	$13-$17
Yellow	$12-$15

1950S COLORS

Chartreuse	$25-$28
Forest Green	$21-$24
Gray	$25-$28
Rose	$26-$29
Medium Green	$55-$68

Place setting with 9" plate, teacup, and saucer, and 6" and 7" plates in yellow. (Note color differences in smaller plates.) **$56-$65/set**

Place setting with 9" plate, teacup, and saucer, and 6" and 7" plates in light green. **$57-$67/set**

Place setting with 9" plate, teacup, and saucer, and 6" and 7" plates in red. **$78-$94/set**

Place setting with 9" plate, teacup, and saucer, and 6" and 7" plates in cobalt blue. **$70-$83/set**

Place setting with 9" plate, teacup, and saucer, and 6" and 7" plates in turquoise. (Note ring pattern variation in large plate.) **$58-$65/set**

Place setting with 9" plate, teacup, and saucer, and 6" and 7" plates in medium green.
$178-$211/set

Place setting with 9" plate, teacup, and saucer, and 6" and 7" plates in gray. **$86-$99/set**

fiesta   9" Plate

Place setting with 9" plate, teacup, and saucer, and 6" and 7" plates in rose. **$92-$108/set**

Place setting with 9" plate, teacup, and saucer, and 6" and 7" plates in chartreuse. **$88-$100/set**

Place setting with 9" plate, teacup, and saucer, and 6" and 7" plates in forest green. **$89-$100/set**

Place setting with 9" plate, teacup, and saucer, and 6" and 7" plates in ivory. (Note color differences in smaller plates.) **$68-$80/set**

fiesta   9" Plate

9" plate in red. **$18-$20**

9" plate in medium green. **$55-$68** (Note color and ring pattern variation between this and the 10" plate.)

9" plate in cobalt blue. **$17-$19**

9" plate in turquoise. **$13-$17**

9" plate in light green. **$12-$15**

VINTAGE FIESTA PIECES

fiesta   10" Plate

A bit more difficult to find, 10" dinner plates can really enhance a basic dinnerware service. Before you purchase a plate, check for scratches. The 10" plate often bears the "Genuine Fiesta" stamp when marked. Production of red examples was halted in 1944 and resumed in 1959.

10" plate in turquoise. **$35-$46**

DEGREE OF DIFFICULTY

1-2

DIMENSIONS:

Actual diameter 10-1/2" by 3/4" thick

PRODUCTION DATES:

1936 to 1969

ORIGINAL COLORS		1950S COLORS	
Cobalt Blue	$40-$46	Chartreuse	$50-$55
Ivory	$40-$46	Forest Green	$50-$56
Light Green	$35-$46	Gray	$45-$50
Red	$40-$48	Rose	$50-$55
Turquoise	$35-$46		
Yellow	$35-$45	Medium Green	$140-$165

Group of 10" plates in all 11 colors. Sold at auction in October 2006 for **$200.**

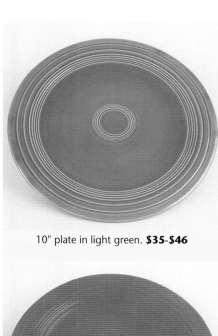

10" plate in light green. **$35-$46**

10" plate in medium green. **$140-$165**

10" plate in ivory. **$40-$46**

10" plate in red. **$40-$48**

10" plate in yellow. **$35-$45**

10" plate in cobalt blue. **$40-$46**

fiesta — Cake plate

One of the hardest pieces of Fiesta to locate, the cake plate is often mistaken for a dinner plate and may be hidden in a stack of dinner plates at an antiques store. Bands of rings appear on the back of the cake plate, the most of any single Fiesta piece. For many collectors, the cake plate and the nestled bowl lids are the centerpieces of their Fiesta collections. Some cake plates have been found with a "Royal Chrome Colored Ovenware" sticker and may have had a separate pierced metal base. No turquoise cake plate has ever been found.

DEGREE OF DIFFICULTY

5

DIMENSIONS:

10-3/8" diameter by 5/8" thick

PRODUCTION DATES:

Approximately six months in 1937.

COLORS

Cobalt Blue	$1,300-$1,450
Ivory	$1,425-$1,495
Light Green	$1,000-$1,200
Red	$1,400-$1,495
Yellow	$1,200-$1,300

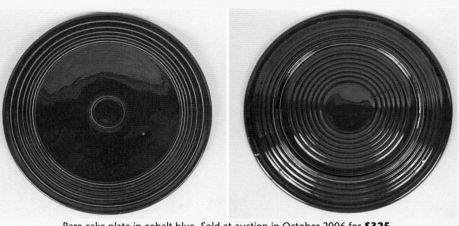

Rare cake plate in cobalt blue. Sold at auction in October 2006 for **$325.**

Photo courtesy Strawser Auctions

Top, bottom, and side views of a cake plate in yellow. **$1,200-$1,300**.

Notice the back of the cake plate is full of rings, unlike the back of a dinner plate, and it is completely flat.

Photo courtesy Strawser Auctions

Rare cake plate in light green. Sold at auction in October 2006 for **$400.**

VINTAGE FIESTA PIECES

Calendar plate

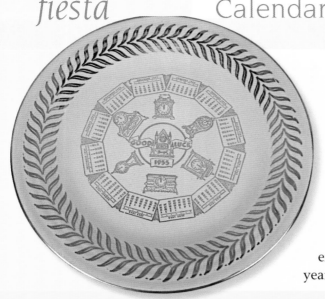

Over the years, many china companies have made calendar plates, and the Homer Laughlin Company was no exception. The company used various blanks (undecorated plates) on which to display the complete calendar for the year. During 1954 and 1955, the blanks that were used were Fiesta plates. A 10" ivory Fiesta plate was used in 1954. In 1955 both 9" and 10" Fiesta plates were utilized. The 10" plates were available in light green, yellow, and ivory. The 9" plates seem to have been made only in ivory. There is no clear explanation for why these plates were made for only two years. None has a manufacturer's mark.

DEGREE OF DIFFICULTY

2-3

DIMENSIONS:

9" and 10" diameter

PRODUCTION DATES:

1954 to 1955

COLORS

Light Green, Ivory, and Yellow
Either size plate   **$40-$50**

The calendar plate is one of the hardest pieces of Fiesta to find.

10" 1954 calendar plate in ivory. Sold at auction in October 2006 for **$5.**

Photo courtesy Strawser Auctions

Photo courtesy Strawser Auctions

10" 1954 calendar plate in ivory. Sold at auction in October 2006 for **$10.**

Photo courtesy Strawser Auctions

10" 1955 calendar plate in ivory. Sold at auction in October 2006 for **$25.**

VINTAGE FIESTA PIECES

fiesta 13" Chop plate

A large round plate like the dinner plate, only larger, the 13" chop may or may not have two different footed rings on the underside. This is due to the fact that the added ring gives additional strength and support to the piece. Some 13" chop plates have been found with a metal Lazy Susan turner. The metal piece fits perfectly under the chop plate, turning it into a great buffet server. The 13" chop plate is often stamped "Genuine Fiesta," though some are unmarked. A raffia-wrapped metal handle was offered as a special promotion and could be clipped onto the plate. (See Promotional Items) Production of red was halted in 1944 and resumed in 1959.

DEGREE OF DIFFICULTY

1-2 for all colors except medium green, which ranks 3-4.

DIMENSIONS:

Actual diameter 12-1/2" by 1-1/8" thick

PRODUCTION DATES:

1936 to 1969

ORIGINAL COLORS		1950S COLORS	
Cobalt Blue	$50-$55	Chartreuse	$85-$90
Ivory	$49-$55	Forest Green	$90-$95
Light Green	$40-$50	Gray	$90-$98
Red	$50-$58	Rose	$85-$90
Turquoise	$45-$49		
Yellow	$40-$48	Medium Green	$450-$525

13" chop plate in medium green. **$450-$525**

13" chop plate in yellow. **$40-$48**

13" chop plate in rose. **$85-$90**

13" chop plate in ivory. **$49-$55**

13" chop plate in light green. **$40-$50**

Photo courtesy Strawser Auctions

13" chop plate in forest green. Sold at auction in October 2006 for **$45.**

Photo courtesy Strawser Auctions

13" chop plate group in the six original colors. Sold at auction in October 2006 for **$95.**

13" chop plate in turquoise. **$45-$49**

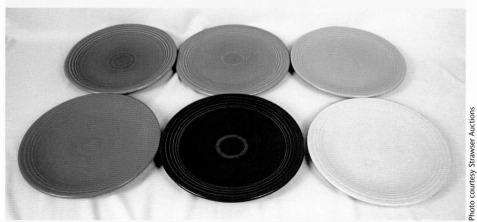

Photo courtesy Strawser Auctions

13" chop plate group in the six original colors. Sold at auction in October 2006 for **$90.**

VINTAGE FIESTA PIECES

15" chop plate in forest green. Sold at auction in October 2006 for **$75.**

The 15" chop plate is excellent for serving a large portion of meat, such as a turkey or ham. Unfortunately, even without anything on it, the piece is heavy. It's a great addition to a buffet table, but should not be passed at a sit-down dinner because of its weight. Fifteen-inch chop plates have a double foot ring, which—with the addition of a metal Lazy Susan turner— transforms this piece into a multi-purpose server. Fifteen-inch chop plates are stamped "Genuine Fiesta." They often have significant surface scratching, which is most evident on dark glazes. Production of red was halted in 1944 and resumed in 1959.

DEGREE OF DIFFICULTY

1-2 for the six original colors, and 2-3 for colors of the 1950s.

DIMENSIONS:

Actual diameter 14-1/4" by 1-1/8" thick

PRODUCTION DATES:

1936 to 1959

ORIGINAL COLORS		1950S COLORS	
Cobalt Blue	$94-$105	Chartreuse	$120-$140
Ivory	$90-$100	Forest Green	$120-$140
Light Green	$60-$75	Gray	$130-$150
Red	$90-$100	Rose	$120-$155
Turquoise	$74-$80		
Yellow	$68-$80		

15" chop plate in rose. Sold at auction in October 2006 for **$65.**

15" chop plate in light green. Sold at auction in October 2006 for **$35.**

15" chop plate in cobalt blue, **$94-$105**, with ivory bud vase, **$100-$120**.

15" chop plate in ivory, **$90-$100**, with light green bud vase, **$85-$94**.

15" chop plate in red, **$90-$100**, with yellow bud vase, **$85-$92**.

15" chop plate in yellow. Sold at auction in October 2006 for **$45**.

VINTAGE FIESTA PIECES

fiesta   10-1/2" Compartment plate

10-1/2" compartment plate in red. **$65-$75**

The 10-1/2" compartment plate appeared in the Fiesta line approximately 15 months after the introduction of Fiesta. It replaced the 12" version because it was much easier to hold and it weighed less. The divisions between the compartments are slightly higher than those of its 12" cousin. It is routinely stamped "Genuine Fiesta." Production of red was halted in 1944 and resumed in 1959.

DEGREE OF DIFFICULTY

2

DIMENSIONS:

10-1/2" diameter by 7/8" thick

PRODUCTION DATES:

1937 to 1959

ORIGINAL COLORS

Cobalt Blue	$50-$60
Ivory	$40-$48
Light Green	$40-$48
Red	$65-$75
Turquoise	$45-$55
Yellow	$40-$48

1950S COLORS

Chartreuse	$75-$82
Forest Green	$85-$95
Gray	$80-$85
Rose	$75-$85

10-1/2" compartment plate in red, **$65-$75**, and 12" compartment plate in light green, **$58-$65.**

10-1/2" compartment plate in ivory. Sold at auction in October 2006 for **$10.**

10-1/2" compartment plate in forest green. Sold at auction in October 2006 for **$35.**

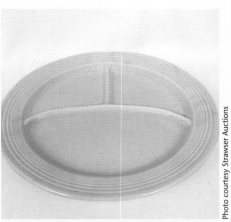

10-1/2" compartment plate in gray. Sold at auction in October 2006 for **$20.**

10-1/2" compartment plate in rose. Sold at auction in October 2006 for **$20.**

10-1/2" compartment plate in cobalt blue. Sold at auction in October 2006 for **$15.**

10-1/2" compartment plate in turquoise. Sold at auction in October 2006 for **$15.**

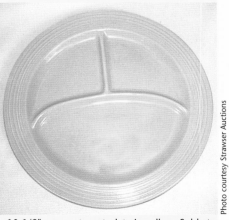

10-1/2" compartment plate in yellow. Sold at auction in October 2006 for **$15.**

VINTAGE FIESTA PIECES

12" Compartment plate

12" compartment
plate in light green.
$58-$65

The 12" compartment plate is also known as a grill plate. It was popular in the 1930s to offer a grill plate in a dinnerware line. Due to the heavy nature of this piece, there are two double-ringed feet underneath. A plate this size had a tendency to warp when it was fired in the kiln. The 12" compartment plate is not marked, and the compartments are slightly shallower than the 10-1/2" size. Because this piece was discontinued in early 1937, it was never made in turquoise.

DEGREE OF DIFFICULTY

2

DIMENSIONS:

Actual diameter 11-3/4" by 1-1/8" thick

PRODUCTION DATES:

1936 to early 1937

COLORS

Cobalt Blue	**$72-$80**
Ivory	**$70-$78**
Light Green	**$58-$65**
Red	**$75-$80**
Yellow	**$58-$65**

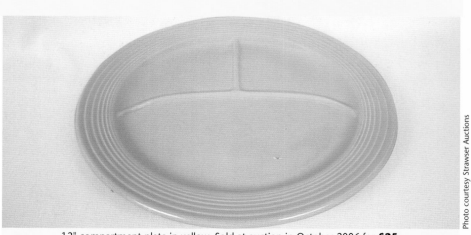

12" compartment plate in yellow. Sold at auction in October 2006 for **$25.**

Photo courtesy Strawser Auctions

12" compartment plate in cobalt blue. **$72-$80**

The 12" compartment plate is also known as a grill plate.

12" compartment plate in red. **$75-$80**

fiesta   Deep plate

Deep plate in rose. **$55-$60**

Also known as a rimmed soup bowl, the deep plate was in production for approximately 33 years and sold quite well, as is evident by the number of them on the market today. Bowls were popular during the Depression because soup was a hearty, filling, and inexpensive way to feed a family. Most dinnerware lines of the 1930s had several size bowls, from dessert to fruit, and from cream soups to large, hearty appetite bowls. Many collectors today use this deep plate as an individual salad bowl. The deep plate is stamped "Genuine Fiesta." Production of red examples was halted in 1944 and resumed in 1959.

DEGREE OF DIFFICULTY

1-2

DIMENSIONS:
8-1/2" diameter by 1-1/2" thick

PRODUCTION DATES:
1936 to 1969

ORIGINAL COLORS		1950S COLORS	
Cobalt Blue	$60-$70	Chartreuse	$50-$55
Ivory	$58-$68	Forest Green	$50-$56
Light Green	$45-$56	Gray	$52-$58
Red	$60-$70	Rose	$55-$60
Turquoise	$45-$54		
Yellow	$45-$55	Medium Green	$135-$150

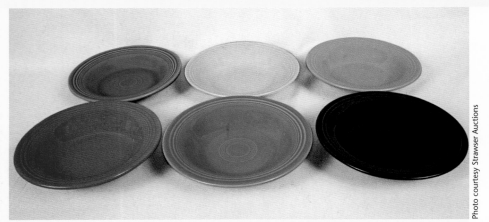

Deep plate group in all six original colors. Sold at auction in October 2006 for **$120.**

Photo courtesy Strawser Auctions

Deep plate in turquoise. **$45-$54**

Deep plate in cobalt blue. **$60-$70**

Deep plate in ivory. **$58-$68**

Deep plate in medium green. **$135-$150**

Deep plate in red. **$60-$70**

Deep plate in yellow. **$45-$55**

Deep plate in chartreuse. **$50-$55**

Deep plate in an unusually strong light green glaze. **$45-$56**

Deep plate group of four in forest green, gray, rose, and chartreuse. Sold at auction in October 2006 for **$130.**

Photo courtesy Strawser Auctions

VINTAGE FIESTA PIECES

Platters

Oval platter

The oval platter was another popular item for Fiesta as well as other dinnerware lines. The angled sides made this an easy item to pass from person to person at the table, as juices would not drip off. Sometime during 1947, the oval platter was revised and made 1/4" shorter. It is commonly marked with a "Genuine Fiesta" stamp. Production of red examples was halted in 1944 and resumed in 1959.

DEGREE OF DIFFICULTY

2

DIMENSIONS:

12-3/4" long before 1947; 12-1/2" long after 1947; 1-1/2" thick

PRODUCTION DATES:

1938 to 1969

ORIGINAL COLORS		1950S COLORS	
Cobalt Blue	$48-$53	Chartreuse	$50-$60
Ivory	$45-$50	Forest Green	$55-$65
Light Green	$40-$46	Gray	$58-$65
Red	$55-$65	Rose	$53-$59
Turquoise	$40-$48		
Yellow	$40-$46	Medium Green	$175-$210

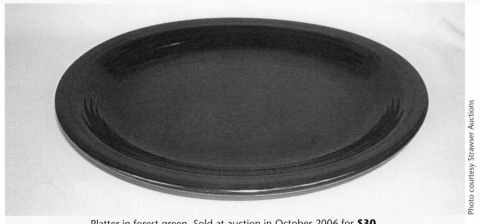

Platter in forest green. Sold at auction in October 2006 for **$30.**

Photo courtesy Strawser Auctions

Oval platter in medium green. **$175-$210**

Oval platter in turquoise. **$40-$48**

Oval platter in chartreuse. **$50-$60**

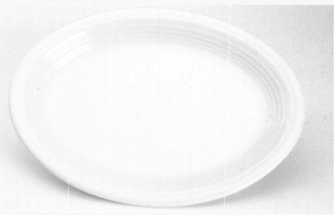

Oval platter in ivory. **$45-$50**

Platter in red. Sold at auction in October 2006 for **$20.**

Photo courtesy Strawser Auctions

VINTAGE FIESTA PIECES

Oval platter

Platter in gray. Sold at auction in October 2006 for **$5.**

Oval platter in cobalt blue. **$48-$53**

Platter in rose. Sold at auction in October 2006 for **$35.**

Photo courtesy Strawser Auctions

Oval platter in light green. **$40-$46**

Salt & Pepper Shakers

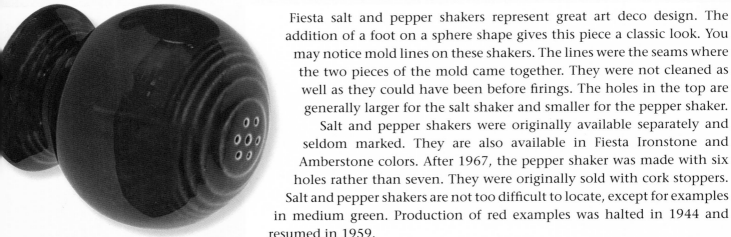

Fiesta salt and pepper shakers represent great art deco design. The addition of a foot on a sphere shape gives this piece a classic look. You may notice mold lines on these shakers. The lines were the seams where the two pieces of the mold came together. They were not cleaned as well as they could have been before firings. The holes in the top are generally larger for the salt shaker and smaller for the pepper shaker. Salt and pepper shakers were originally available separately and seldom marked. They are also available in Fiesta Ironstone and Amberstone colors. After 1967, the pepper shaker was made with six holes rather than seven. They were originally sold with cork stoppers. Salt and pepper shakers are not too difficult to locate, except for examples in medium green. Production of red examples was halted in 1944 and resumed in 1959.

DEGREE OF DIFFICULTY

1 for the six original colors,
1-2 for colors of the 1950s, and
3-4 for medium green.

DIMENSIONS:

2-3/8" by 2-3/4"

PRODUCTION DATES:

1936 to 1969

ORIGINAL COLORS		1950S COLORS	
Cobalt Blue	$30-$34/pair	Chartreuse	$50-$55/pair
Ivory	$29-$35/pair	Forest Green	$50-$55/pair
Light Green	$25-$29/pair	Gray	$48-$52/pair
Red	$30-$35/pair	Rose	$48-$52/pair
Turquoise	$25-$29/pair		
Yellow	$25-$29/pair	Medium Green	$200-$210/pair

Group of salt and pepper shakers, some with minor nicks. Sold at auction in October 2006 for **$50.**

Photo courtesy Strawser Auctions

Shakers in forest green. Sold at auction in October 2006 for **$25/pair.**

Photo courtesy Strawser Auctions

Shakers in medium green. **$200-$210/pair**

Shakers in light green. **$25-$29/pair**

Shakers in red. **$30-$35/pair**

Shakers in turquoise (note color variation). **$25-$29/pair**

Shakers in cobalt blue. **$30-$34/pair**

VINTAGE FIESTA PIECES

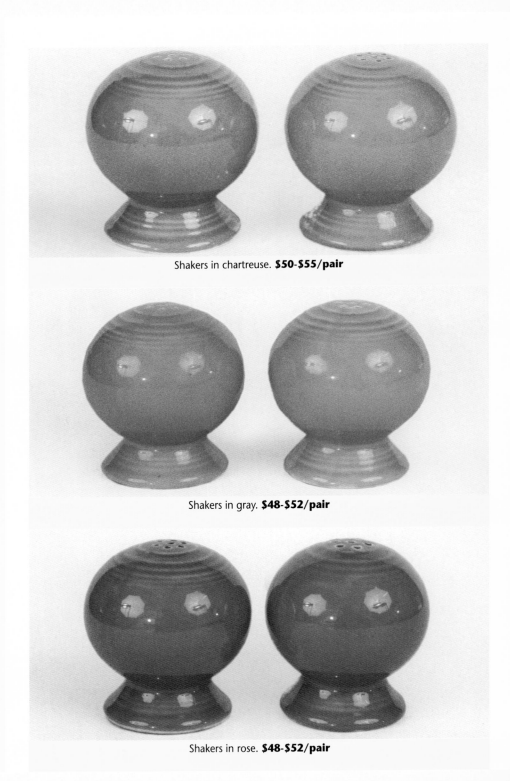

Shakers in chartreuse. **$50-$55/pair**

Shakers in gray. **$48-$52/pair**

Shakers in rose. **$48-$52/pair**

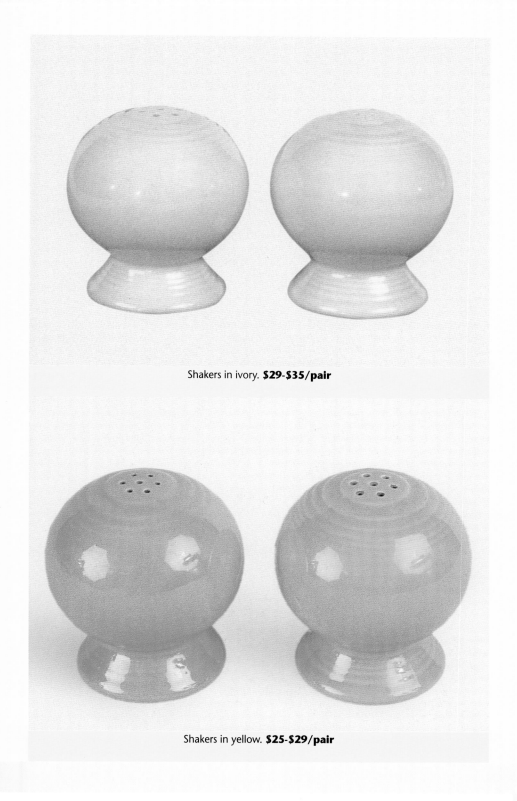

Shakers in ivory. **$29-$35/pair**

Shakers in yellow. **$25-$29/pair**

Sauceboats

The sauceboat (also called a gravy boat) came out in 1938, but the under plate, which looks like a mini oval platter, was not produced until 1969. For those of you without an under plate, a gravy ladle works well and prevents dripping. This piece was part of the vintage line (marked "Fiesta/HLC U.S.A." or "Fiesta/Made in U.S.A."), and is available in the Ironstone colors (unmarked) and in the Post-'86 line. Production of red was halted in 1944 and resumed in 1959.

DEGREE OF DIFFICULTY

1-2 for all colors other than medium green, which ranks 3-4.

DIMENSIONS:

4-7/8" by 8" by 4-1/2"

PRODUCTION DATES:

1938 to 1969

ORIGINAL COLORS		1950S COLORS	
Cobalt Blue	$70-$79	Chartreuse	$70-$80
Ivory	$70-$79	Forest Green	$72-$84
Light Green	$50-$60	Gray	$70-$82
Red	$75-$89	Rose	$75-$85
Turquoise	$50-$54		
Yellow	$50-$54	Medium Green	$195-$240

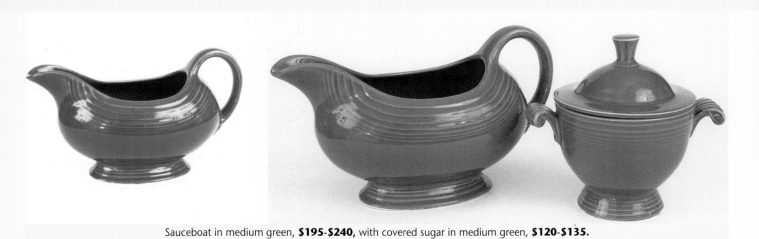

Sauceboat in medium green, **$195-$240,** with covered sugar in medium green, **$120-$135.**

Sauceboat in gray. **$70**-**$82**

Sauceboat in forest green. **$72**-**$84**

Sauceboat in rose. Sold at auction in October 2006 for **$30.**

Photo courtesy Strawser Auctions

Sauceboat in yellow. **$50**-**$54**

Sauceboat in ivory. **$70**-**$79**

Sauceboat in turquoise. **$50**-**$54**

Sauceboat in light green. **$50-$60**

Compote in cobalt blue, **$85-$95,** with sauceboat in light green, **$50-$60.**

Sauceboat in cobalt blue. **$70-$79**

Sauceboat and under plate in red. **$75-$89** for the sauceboat only.

Teapots

Medium teapot

The medium teapot made its debut one year after the introduction of Fiesta. While somewhat similar to the large teapot, there are several differences. On the medium teapot, the lid finial does not flare; the spout is longer and arched; and the handle is C-shaped rather than shaped like a ring. The vent holes were put in by hand, so watch for some variations on the lid—some lids may not even have a vent hole. Made for 32 years, medium teapots in the original colors are much easier to find than large teapots, which were produced for only 11 years. Medium teapots in the colors of the 1950s are harder to find, but it's the last color, medium green, that tops the charts in terms of dollars. Production of red examples was halted in 1944 and resumed in 1959.

DEGREE OF DIFFICULTY

2 for the six original colors and 3 for the colors of the 1950s and medium green.

DIMENSIONS:

8-1/2" by 5-1/8" with lid, by 5-5/8"

PRODUCTION DATES:

1937 to 1969

ORIGINAL COLORS		1950S COLORS	
Cobalt Blue	$210-$235	Chartreuse	$300-$325
Ivory	$195-$220	Forest Green	$325-$340
Light Green	$160-$175	Gray	$350-$375
Red	$200-$230	Rose	$275-$295
Turquoise	$175-$200		
Yellow	$160-$180	Medium Green	$1,475-$1,595

Medium teapot in yellow. **$160-$180**

Medium teapot in red. **$200-$230**

Medium teapot in ivory. **$195-$220**

Medium teapot in chartreuse. Sold at auction in October 2006 for **$160.**

Medium teapot in turquoise. **$175-$200**

Medium teapot in rose. **$275-$295**

Medium teapot in forest green. Sold at auction in October 2006 for **$150.**

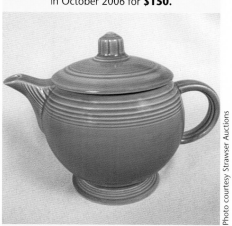

Medium teapot in light green. Sold at auction in October 2006 for **$85.**

Medium teapot in medium green. **$1,475-$1,595**

Photo courtesy Strawser Auctions

fiesta Large teapot

Large teapot in yellow. **$290-$300**

This is one of the many items that were in the line when Fiesta debuted in January 1936. It is not known why a smaller-sized teapot (called the medium teapot) with a different handle was introduced a year later, but the shear bulk of the large teapot when it is full, along with its somewhat awkward ring handle, may be the reason. Although a beautiful design, it is difficult to pour when filled with eight cups of hot water. The large teapot may be marked either "Fiesta/HLC USA" or "Made in USA." The lids typically have a steam vent hole, which was applied by hand. Like all things hand-done, the hole may be close to the finial or near the edge. Production of red examples was halted in 1944.

DEGREE OF DIFFICULTY

2-3

DIMENSIONS:

9-1/4" by 6-3/4" with lid, by 6-1/8

PRODUCTION DATES:

1936 to 1946

COLORS

Color	Price
Cobalt Blue	$350-$375
Ivory	$325-$345
Light Green	$275-$295
Red	$350-$365
Turquoise	$295-$315
Yellow	$290-$300

Large teapot in turquoise. Sold at auction in October 2006 for **$95**.

Large teapot in light green. Sold at auction in October 2006 for **$75**.

Photo courtesy Strawser Auctions

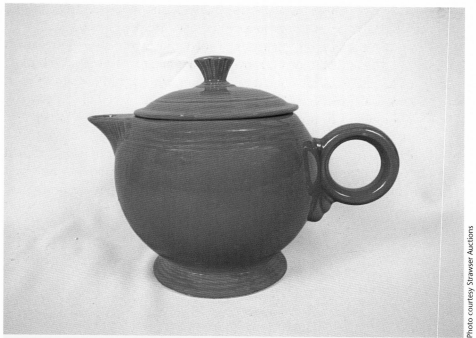

Photo courtesy Strawser Auctions

Large teapot in red. Sold at auction in October 2006 for **$150.**

Photo courtesy Strawser Auctions

Large teapot in cobalt blue. Sold at auction in October 2006 for **$80.**

VINTAGE PIECES

Trays

Relish tray

Relish tray with removable metal handle.

The Fiesta relish tray (the base, four quarter-round inserts, and a round center section) was shipped from the Homer Laughlin Co. in one color. Some retailers and buyers mixed up their colors to create various color schemes. During its 11 years of production, the tray's quarter-round inserts were made two different ways. Because of this, there is a slight difference in the length and width of the pieces. Be aware that if you are buying sections at different times from different people that they may not all fit together inside a relish tray. The tray is typically marked "Fiesta/HLC USA" while the inserts may be unmarked, or marked "Genuine Fiesta/Made in USA." Production of red was discontinued in 1944.

DEGREE OF DIFFICULTY

2-3

OVERALL DIMENSIONS:

Tray (with five inserts) 10-7/8" by 1-1/2"

PRODUCTION DATES:

1936 to 1946

COLORS

Cobalt Blue	**$300-$335/set**
Ivory	**$325-$350/set**
Light Green	**$295-$310/set**
Red	**$325-$355/set**
Turquoise	**$300-$340/set**
Yellow	**$290-$310/set**

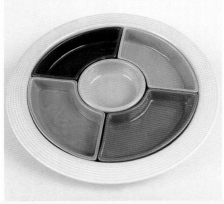

Relish tray in ivory with cobalt blue, light green, red, turquoise, and yellow inserts.

Relish tray in light green with cobalt blue, ivory, turquoise, and yellow inserts.

Relish tray and inserts in light green, as it would have come from the factory. **$295-$310/set**

Tidbit tray

Tidbit trays are found in two- and three-tier versions in both original and 1950s color variations. There are no official records of HLC making these as actual pieces, but there is evidence it made some of the original holed plates for construction of the trays. The trays that were drilled at the factory will have glaze inside the holes. Others with white holes were drilled and assembled post-factory (the hardware was and still is readily available). The tops came several ways over the years, either with a large ring handle or an inverted triangle.

Current suggested price: $100-$200 (lower end for cobalt blue, light green, yellow, ivory, and turquoise; higher end for red, forest green, chartreuse, rose, gray, and medium green)

Tidbit tray in rose, chartreuse, and yellow. Sold at auction in October 2006 for **$30.**

Photo courtesy Strawser Auctions

Tidbit tray in ivory, light green, and cobalt blue. **$100-$200**

fiesta   Utility tray

This tray was a utilitarian piece used for a variety of functions: a base for the sugar and creamer or the salt and pepper set, or as a plate for pickles, olives, or celery. There are two slight variations to this tray. The original had a narrow, unglazed foot and straight sides. The second variation, introduced in 1938, had more slanted sides and a glazed foot (note a set of three pin marks equidistant from each other that form a triangle). The latter version is typically marked "Genuine Fiesta/HLC USA." Production of red examples was halted in 1944.

DEGREE OF DIFFICULTY

2

DIMENSIONS:

10-1/2" by 1-1/4

PRODUCTION DATES:

1936 to 1946

COLORS

Cobalt Blue	**$49-$53**
Ivory	**$45-$49**
Light Green	**$42-$47**
Red	**$50-$55**
Turquoise	**$48-$53**
Yellow	**$44-$48**

Utility tray in red. **$50-$55**

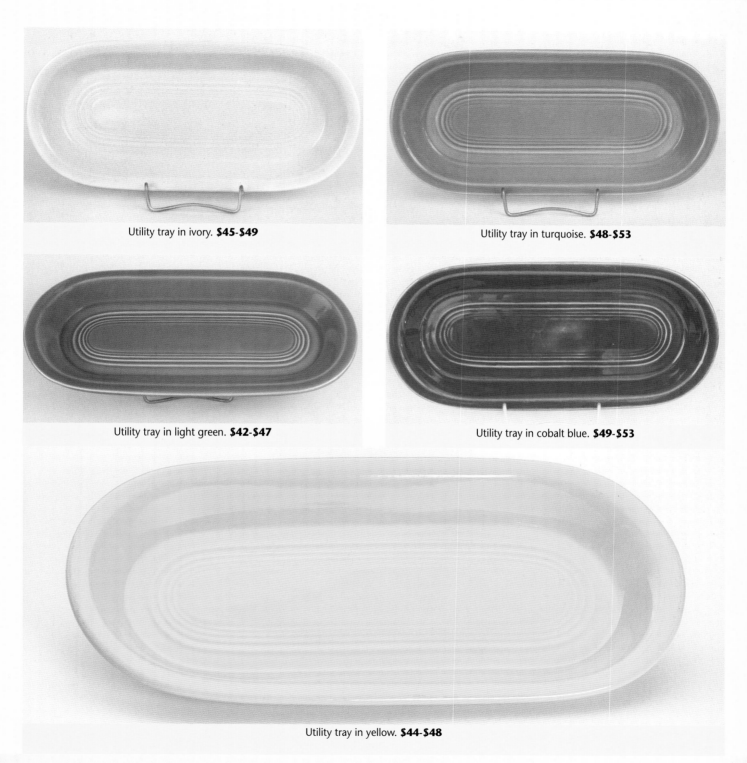

Utility tray in ivory. **$45-$49**

Utility tray in turquoise. **$48-$53**

Utility tray in light green. **$42-$47**

Utility tray in cobalt blue. **$49-$53**

Utility tray in yellow. **$44-$48**

Tumblers

Water tumbler

The water tumbler differs from the juice tumbler in several ways. First and perhaps most obvious is the height—the water tumbler is approximately one inch taller. The water tumbler's sides flare more and have more pronounced, rounded rings. Unlike juice tumblers, water tumblers are always marked either "Fiesta/HLC USA" or "Made in USA." There may be minute variations in height. Production of red examples was halted in 1944.

DEGREE OF DIFFICULTY

1-2

DIMENSIONS:

4-1/2" by 3-3/8"

PRODUCTION DATES:

1937 to 1946

ORIGINAL COLORS

Cobalt Blue	**$72-$80**
Ivory	**$70-$80**
Light Green	**$65-$68**
Red	**$75-$85**
Turquoise	**$65-$69**
Yellow	**$67-$70**

Water tumbler in light green. **$65-$68**

Water tumbler in red. **$75-$85**

Water tumbler in yellow. **$67-$70**

Three water tumblers in light green, **$65-$68,** cobalt blue, **$72-$80,** and turquoise, **$65-$69.**

JUICE TUMBLER:

See Promotional Items.

Water tumblers in light green, **$65-$68,** yellow, **$67-$70,** and red, **$75-$85.**

VINTAGE PIECES

Vases

Bud vase

Made for slightly over 10 years, the bud vase seems to have sold well during its original run as is evident by how many are for resale today. Vintage pieces may be marked either "Fiesta/HLC USA" or "Fiesta Made in USA." The bud vase is also part of the post-'86 line, with only a minute difference in height. Several other pottery companies made a version similar to this one. Before purchasing, check the vase over carefully. Production of red examples was halted in 1944.

DEGREE OF DIFFICULTY:

1-2

DIMENSIONS:

6-5/16" by 2-7/8"

PRODUCTION DATES:

1936 to 1946

COLORS

Cobalt Blue	$100-$130
Ivory	$100-$120
Light Green	$85-$94
Red	$100-$130
Turquoise	$95-$115
Yellow	$85-$92

Bud vases in turquoise, **$95-$115**, cobalt blue, **$100-$130**, ivory, **$100-$120**, yellow, **$85-$92**, light green, **$85-$94**, and red, **$100-$130**.

Bud vase in cobalt blue. **$100-$130**

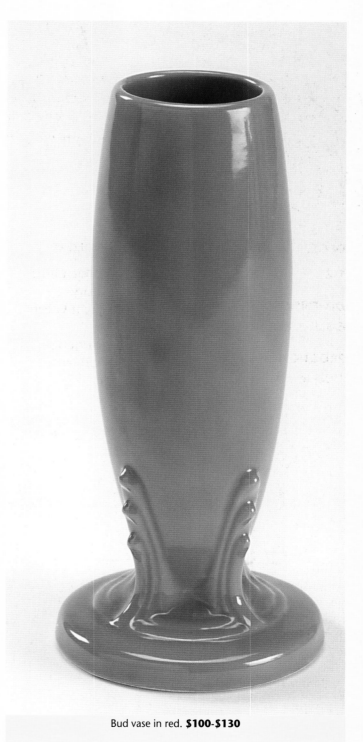

Bud vase in red. **$100-$130**

fiesta   8" Vase

The 8" vase was produced for approximately 10 years—four years longer than the 10" and 12" vases. Because red was discontinued in 1944, 8" vases in that color are slightly harder to find. The 8" vase may be marked either "Fiesta/HLC USA" or "Fiesta Made in USA." There are minute height variations in all three sizes.

8" vase in yellow.
$570-$640

DEGREE OF DIFFICULTY

2-3

DIMENSIONS:

7-15/16" by 4"

PRODUCTION DATES:

1936 to 1946

COLORS

Cobalt Blue	**$725-$775**
Ivory	**$740-$780**
Light Green	**$550-$635**
Red	**$760-$800**
Turquoise	**$600-$650**
Yellow	**$570-$640**

8" vase in ivory. **$740-$780**

8" vases in turquoise, **$600-$650**, red, **$760-$800**, and yellow, **$570-$640**.

8" vase in light green. Sold at auction in October 2006 for **$300.**

8" vase in cobalt blue. Sold at auction in October 2006 for **$475.**

Grouping of vases in a variety of colors.

VINTAGE PIECES

The 10" vase (like the 12" version) was in production for six years and is marked "Fiesta HLC USA" in the mold. You may find mold lines along the sides of these vases because they were made with a four-part mold. Light green and yellow are slightly less desirable than the other four colors. There are minute height variations in all three sizes.

DEGREE OF DIFFICULTY

3

DIMENSIONS:
10" by 5-1/8"

PRODUCTION DATES:
1936 to 1942

COLORS

Cobalt Blue	$925-$990
Ivory	$975-$1,000
Light Green	$900-$975
Red	$1,000-$1,100
Turquoise	$900-$975
Yellow	$900-$975

10" vase in turquoise. Sold at auction in October 2006 for **$475.**

Photo courtesy Strawser Auctions

Three vases—12", 10", and 8"—in red. **$2,000-$2,100, $1,000-$1,100,** and **$760-$800,** respectively.

VINTAGE PIECES

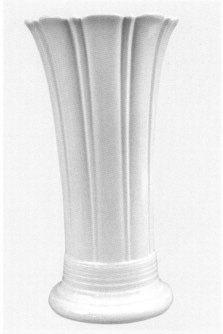

10" vase in ivory. **$975-$1,000**

10" vase in cobalt blue. Sold at auction in
October 2006 for **$550.**

Photo courtesy Strawser Auctions

10" vase in light green. **$900-$975**

VINTAGE PIECES

fiesta 12" Vase

One of the most expensive items in the line, the 12" vase is a centerpiece of any vintage Fiesta collection. Expect to pay $2,000 for one in red. Like the 10" vase, the 12" vase was produced for six years and is typically marked "Fiesta/HLC USA." There are minute height variations in all three sizes.

DEGREE OF DIFFICULTY

3

DIMENSIONS:

11-3/4" by 5-15/16"

PRODUCTION DATES:

1936 to 1942

COLORS

Cobalt Blue	**$1,300-$1,500**
Ivory	**$1,150-$1,200**
Light Green	**$1,100-$1,200**
Red	**$2,000-$2,100**
Turquoise	**$1,300-$1,450**
Yellow	**$1,100-$1,200**

12" vase in red. Sold at auction in October 2006 for **$850.**

Photo courtesy Strawser Auctions

Left to right: 8", 10", and 12" vases in turquoise, yellow, and cobalt blue. **$600-$650, $875-$900,** and **$1,300-$1,500,** respectively.

12" vase in turquoise. Sold at auction in October 2006 for **$600.**

Photo courtesy Strawser Auctions

12" vase in yellow. Sold at auction in October 2006 for **$600.**

Photo courtesy Strawser Auctions

12" vase in light green. **$1,100-$1,200.**

fiesta Promotional Items

For approximately three years, between 1940 and 1943, retailers were offered a series of special Fiesta pieces that could retail for $1. Some retailers took advantage of this promotion by selling these special items at that price, while some sold them at either a reduced price of 75 cents or for upwards of $1.25. This was a great way for people to supplement their Fiesta sets—or for those who did not own any Fiesta dinnerware to get their feet wet—for a small amount of money. By doing this, many people began to acquire more Fiesta over the coming months.

The seven promotional items were:

Salad set–Yellow "unlisted" salad bowl with a red spoon and light green fork

French casserole–Yellow

Sugar, creamer and tray set–Yellow sugar bowl and creamer on a cobalt blue tray

Juice set–Yellow pitcher with six juice glasses, one in each of the six original colors

Chop plate with metal handle

Covered casserole with pie plate–light green casserole bottom, red lid, and yellow pie plate.

Refrigerator set–Three bowls, one each in light green, cobalt blue, and yellow, and a lid in red

"Unlisted" or promotional salad bowl (set)

Collectors have dubbed this bowl the "unlisted" salad bowl as it never appeared on any company price lists. These bowls were sold along with a Kitchen Kraft fork and spoon, thus becoming the promotional salad set (see Kitchen Kraft). Although the bowls were usually yellow, a rare few have been found in light green, ivory, and cobalt blue. There are no interior rings on the bowls, and the impressed mark is "Fiesta/Made in USA/HLCo."

Unlisted salad bowl in yellow. **$100-$125**

DEGREE OF DIFFICULTY

2-3 for yellow, 5 for cobalt blue.

DIMENSIONS:

9-3/4" by 3-1/2"

PRODUCTION DATES:

1940 to 1943

COLORS

Cobalt Blue	$3,100-$3,300
Yellow	$100-$120

Front: 11-3/4" fruit bowl in yellow with experimental spoon in turquoise. Back: Promotional salad bowl in cobalt blue, **$3,100-$3,300,** with experimental spoon in ivory.

Promotional salad bowl in cobalt blue, **$3,100-$3,300,** with red spoon and yellow fork. This was the Promotional Salad Set that sold for approximately three years.

fiesta French Casserole

The French casserole resembles a skillet with cover. You will also find its somewhat unusual stick handle repeated on the first creamer, the after dinner coffeepot, and the after dinner coffee cup (also called the demitasse cup). The French casserole is not easy to find, and often you will encounter either the top or bottom. If you come across a yellow lid, an easy way to tell if it is for the French casserole or the regular casserole is to check the underside. If it has a band of four rings, it is the regular casserole lid. Another way to determine which lid you have is to check the finial. The regular casserole has a finial that flares out more. Before purchasing, check the handle for cracks and chips. Because of the long awkward handle, many have become damaged over the years. Marked "Fiesta/Made in USA."

French casserole in yellow with yellow cover.
$275-$325

DEGREE OF DIFFICULTY

4

DIMENSIONS:

11-3/4" by 4-1/4"

PRODUCTION DATES:

1940 to 1943

COLORS

Yellow   **$275-$325**

Yellow French casserole lid, red covered casserole lid, and standard yellow French casserole bottom with rare light green lid.

Creamer/sugar and tray set

Individual creamer (red), **$325-$375**, and sugar (yellow), **$90-$150**, on a turquoise figure-8 tray, **$450-$495.**

The individual sugar and creamer, along with what collectors refer to as the figure-8 tray, were part of the promotional set. Notice the handles on the sugar and creamer: They are different from the other Fiesta sugar and creamer in that their handles are more of a "C" shape, rather than the round ring handle. They also tend to be lighter in weight.

The standard color combination was cobalt blue for the tray, and yellow for the creamer and sugar (impressed "Fiesta Made in USA"). But other colors, chiefly red and turquoise, have been found. If you find a non-standard color, expect to pay three to four times more for it than for a standard color. Most cobalt blue trays will often show even the slightest surface scratching, caused by the rough, unglazed bottom of the sugar and creamer. Check sugar bowl lids for rim chips.

DEGREE OF DIFFICULTY

3 for yellow sugar and creamer on cobalt blue tray; 4 for red creamer on turquoise tray; and 5 for anything else.

DIMENSIONS:

Creamer (called "the individual"), 4-7/8" by 2-5/8" by 3-5/8"
Sugar Bowl (called "the individual"), 5-1/4" by 3-1/2" by 3-5/8"
Tray (figure-8), 10-3/8" by 5" by 7/8"

PRODUCTION DATES:

1940 to 1943

COLORS

Red creamer	**$325-$375**	Yellow creamer or sugar bowl
Cobalt Blue tray	**$100-$150**	**$90-$150 each**
		Turquoise tray **$450-$495**

Figure-8 tray in turquoise with a glaze flaw that is typical of pieces with this glaze. **$450-$495**

Promotional creamer and sugar in yellow, **$90-$150 each**, with cobalt blue figure-8 tray, **$100-$150.**

Promotional creamer in red, **$325-$375**, on tray in turquoise, **$450-$495**—hard to find colors for these items.

fiesta Juice tumbler

Juice tumblers were made for special promotions in 1948 (called "Jubilee"), in about 1951 (for the Woolworth's "Rhythm" line that included Harlequin yellow), and as a promotion for Old Reliable Coffee. The tumblers were part of a seven-piece set that included the disk juice pitcher in gray (rare), red, turquoise (very rare), and both Fiesta and Harlequin yellow. There is a slight difference in the height and thickness of the juice tumbler, which holds approximately five ounces of liquid. Seldom marked, they may have an "HLCo USA" stamp.

DEGREE OF DIFFICULTY

1-2 for six original colors,
3 for rose and gray, and
4 for forest green and chartreuse

DIMENSIONS:

3-1/2" by 2-1/2"

PRODUCTION DATES:

1940 to 1943 (re-released in 1948 and again in 1951 in other colors)

ORIGINAL COLORS

Cobalt Blue	$50-$56
Ivory	$50-$55
Light Green	$45-$48
Red	$55-$60
Turquoise	$45-$48
Yellow	$45-$48

1950S COLORS

Chartreuse	$800-$875
Forest Green	$800-$850
Gray	$230-$250
Rose	$65-$75

Six Fiesta juice tumblers in yellow, turquoise, red, cobalt blue, ivory, and light green, plus a Fiesta juice tumbler in Harlequin rose.

Juice tumbler in cobalt blue. **$50-$56**

Juice tumbler in yellow. **$45-$48**

Juice tumbler in red. **$55-$60**

Juice tumbler in light green. **$45-$48**

Juice tumbler in turquoise. **$45-$48**

Juice tumbler in ivory. **$50-$55**

Notice the height difference between these juice tumblers in yellow and turquoise.

Notice the difference in the thickness of the sides of these juice tumblers in yellow and turquoise.

Juice tumblers in chartreuse and Harlequin yellow, rose, and turquoise, with a red disk juice pitcher.

Disk juice pitcher

Disk juice pitcher in red. **$500-$580.**

Most juice pitchers are yellow, as this was the standard color chosen for the promotion. Homer Laughlin China Company produced some in red for a special order. The tumblers in this promotion were one each of the first six colors. The difference in price between the yellow and red pitchers reflects the difficulty in obtaining one. During the 1939-1943 promotion, the juice pitcher, plus six tumblers, could be purchased for only $1. Like the larger disk water pitcher, the juice pitcher has flat sides, making it easy to store in the door of your refrigerator. Usually marked "Fiesta/Made in USA."

DEGREE OF DIFFICULTY

1 for yellow, 4 for red.

DIMENSIONS:
6" by 6-1/2" by 3-1/2"

PRODUCTION DATES:
1940 to 1943

COLORS

Red	**$500-$580**
Yellow	**$55-$65**

Three disk juice pitchers: left, yellow, **$55-$65;** center, post-'86 yellow; right, Harlequin yellow; and a mini disk pitcher in post-'86 sunflower.

fiesta

Chop Plate with Metal Handle

A 13" chop plate with a metal clip-on handle made up this promotional item. The handle had raffia wrapping along the top, making it easy to hold and carry. Although the metal handles were not produced by Homer Laughlin China Company, they were shipped along with the chop plates from the company.

A raffia-wrapped metal handle turns this 13" light green chop plate into a serving tray. This was part of the promotional campaign of 1940-1943.

Casserole with pie plate

DEGREE OF DIFFICULTY

2 for the pie plate, 3 for the casserole.

DIMENSIONS:

Casserole–8-1/2", pie plate–9"

PRODUCTION DATES:

1940 to 1943

COLORS

Light green and red casserole and yellow pie plate set: **$210-$235**

A casserole and pie plate made up this $1 promotion. Most of the casserole bottoms are light green, the covers are red, and the 9" pie plates are yellow. This is how the sets were shipped from the factory. However, once they arrived at the retail outlet store, clerks or customers could mix and match to create their own individual color combinations. You could bake and serve in the same piece, thus making it easy for the homemaker of the early 1940s.

Promotional covered casserole with Fiesta red lid and Fiesta green bowl on a Fiesta yellow Kitchen Kraft 9" pie plate. This set in the same color combination was also sold by Royal Metal Manufacturing. **$210-$235**

Refrigerator Set

Another item from the Kitchen Kraft line was the refrigerator set. The set was made up of four pieces—three bowls and a lid. Because the set could be stacked, three separate foods could be stored in one small area, saving space in the smaller-sized refrigerators of the 1930s. Likewise, the design of the piece made it easy to store even one food item. The standard colors for the set were one bowl each in yellow, cobalt blue, and light green with a lid in red.

Kitchen Kraft stacking refrigerator set in yellow with paper label to one unit. Sold at auction in October 2006 for **$110**.

DEGREE OF DIFFICULTY

2

DIMENSIONS:

Lid: 5-1/2" wide
Bowl: 5-1/4" wide x 2-1/4" high

PRODUCTION DATES:

1940 to 1943

COLORS

Cover	**$75-$85**
Bowl	**$45-$55**

Kitchen Kraft stacking refrigerator set in light green with a hairline crack on one unit. Sold at auction in October 2006 for **$85.**

Kitchen Kraft stacking refrigerator set in red. Sold at auction in October 2006 for **$250.**

Kitchen Kraft stacking refrigerator set in cobalt blue with paper label to one unit and minor nicks to two units. Sold at auction in October 2006 for **$125.**

Fiesta Kitchen Kraft

The 20 items produced were:

- Small, medium, and large covered jars
- 6", 8", and 10" mixing bowls
- 8-1/2", 7-1/2", and 4-1/2" covered casseroles
- 10" pie plate
- Large salt and pepper shakers
- 11" cake plate
- 4-piece refrigerator set
- Spoon, fork, and cake server
- Large covered jug
- 6" and 9" plates

Although Fiesta Kitchen Kraft made its debut in mid-1937, it dates back to 1933. At this time Homer Laughlin China Company had a line of oven-to-tableware items under the OvenServe name. The idea was great. A person could bake and serve food in the same vessel, cutting down on the number of items used in the process. And in doing so, the item could go on the table and match the dinnerware service perfectly.

Items in the Fiesta Kitchen Kraft line were produced from 1938 to the mid-1940s, in cobalt blue, light green, red, and yellow, and included 20 pieces. An impressed mark, "Fiesta Kitchen Kraft U.S.A.," and an applied label, "Guaranteed Fiesta Kitchen Kraft U-S-A," were both used. Kitchen Kraft shapes in Fiesta colors were also offered in special promotions for the Royal Metal Manufacturing Company of Chicago, and in combination with regular Fiesta pieces. Some items are not difficult to find, but those with original labels bring a premium.

Fiesta Kitchen Kraft salad fork in yellow with original paper label.

Fiesta Kitchen Kraft individual casserole in light green. **$150-$160**

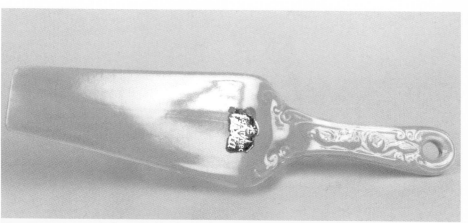

Fiesta Kitchen Kraft cake server in yellow. **$140-$150**

Fiesta Kitchen Kraft cake plate in yellow.
$50-$60

Fiesta Kitchen Kraft cake server in light green. **$140-$150**

Fiesta Kitchen Kraft cake plate in cobalt blue.
$60-$70

Fiesta Kitchen Kraft salad fork with cake server in cobalt blue, **$150-$160.**

fiesta Kitchen Kraft

Fiesta Kitchen Kraft medium covered jar in yellow. **$250-$300**

Fiesta Kitchen Kraft shakers in light green and cobalt blue. **$90-$110**

Kitchen Kraft covered jug in cobalt blue. Sold at auction in October 2006 for **$155**.

Fiesta Kitchen Kraft shakers in red. **$90-$110/pair**

Kitchen Kraft covered jug in light green. Sold at auction in October 2006 for **$100**.

Fiesta Kitchen Kraft refrigerator sets, with three bowls in light green, cobalt blue, and ivory, **$45-$55 each**, and two covers in cobalt blue and red, **$75-$85 each.**

Photo courtesy Strawser Auctions

Photo courtesy Strawser Auctions

FIESTA KITCHEN KRAFT

Kitchen Kraft small mixing bowl in light green. Sold at auction in October 2006 for **$20.**

Kitchen Kraft medium mixing bowl in red. Sold at auction in October 2006 for **$30.**

Kitchen Kraft medium mixing bowl in cobalt blue. Sold at auction in October 2006 for **$25.**

Kitchen Kraft medium mixing bowl in light green, with label. Sold at auction in October 2006 for **$55.**

Kitchen Kraft 10" mixing bowl in rare chartreuse. Sold at auction in October 2006 for **$50.**

Fiesta Kitchen Kraft covered casserole in light green. **$80-$110**

Kitchen Kraft large mixing bowl in cobalt blue. Sold at auction in October 2006 for **$30.**

Royal Metal oval platter in Fiesta red with metal stand. **$135-$150/set**

FIESTA KITCHEN KRAFT

Fiesta Kitchen Kraft salad fork in light green. **$125-$140**

Fiesta Kitchen Kraft salad spoon in light green. **$125-$140**

Fiesta Kitchen Kraft salad spoon in red, never-produced spoon in ivory (rare), never-produced spoon in turquoise (rare), and salad fork in yellow.

Kitchen Kraft platter in cobalt blue with label and chrome holder/carrier. Sold at auction in October 2006 for **$35**.

Kitchen Kraft covered casserole in cobalt blue on a Royal Metal chrome stand. **$130-$140/set**

Two Fiesta Kitchen Kraft covered jars, medium (7"diameter), **$250-$300**, and large (8" diameter) in light green, **$300-$350**, the smaller with original label.

Kitchen Kraft promotional casserole in red with chrome holder/carrier. Sold at auction in October 2006 for **$80**.

9-1/2" pie plates in colors similar to light green and cobalt blue, but actually part of the Zephyr line made by Cronin China Co., Minerva, Ohio, in the 1930s.

Kitchen Kraft 9-1/2" pie plate in Fiesta yellow, left, and 9-1/2" yellow pie plate, part of the Zephyr line made by Cronin China Co., Minerva, Ohio, in the 1930s. (Note difference in rim width.)

FIESTA KITCHEN KRAFT

Pair of Kitchen Kraft range shakers in red. Sold at auction in October 2006 for **$65.**

Pair of Kitchen Kraft range shakers in cobalt blue. Sold at auction in October 2006 for **$70.**

Kitchen Kraft platter in yellow. Sold at auction in October 2006 for **$10.**

Kitchen Kraft platter in red. Sold at auction in October 2006 for **$5.**

Pair of Kitchen Kraft range shakers in yellow. Sold at auction in October 2006 for **$40.**

Fiesta Kitchen Kraft salad spoon in red. **$140-$150**

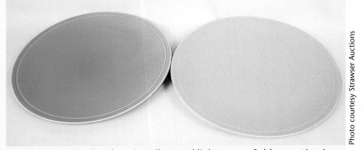

Kitchen Kraft cake plates in yellow and light green. Sold at auction in October 2006 for **$25.**

Fiesta Kitchen Kraft individual casseroles in light green and yellow. **$150-$160 each**

FIESTA KITCHEN KRAFT

Kitchen Kraft large covered jar in red. Sold at auction in October 2006 for **$95.**

Kitchen Kraft medium covered jar in red. Sold at auction in October 2006 for **$145.**

Kitchen Kraft stacking refrigerator set in the rare color of ivory with label on lid and minor nicks to two units. Sold at auction in October 2006 for **$475.**

Kitchen Kraft medium covered jar in red. Sold at auction in October 2006 for **$145.**

Kitchen Kraft small covered jar in light green. Sold at auction in October 2006 for **$85.**

Kitchen Kraft small covered jar in cobalt blue. Sold at auction in October 2006 for **$140.**

Pie plate in blue, part of the Zephyr line made by Cronin China Co., Minerva, Ohio, in the 1930s.

Kitchen Kraft stacking refrigerator set in yellow with paper label to one unit. Sold at auction in October 2006 for **$110.**

FIESTA KITCHEN KRAFT

Tin Kitchenware

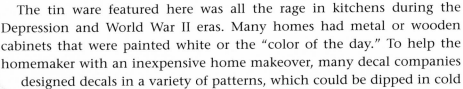

The tin ware featured here was all the rage in kitchens during the Depression and World War II eras. Many homes had metal or wooden cabinets that were painted white or the "color of the day." To help the homemaker with an inexpensive home makeover, many decal companies designed decals in a variety of patterns, which could be dipped in cold water and then applied to just about anything. Baby furniture, bathrooms, and kitchens were the main focal point of this cheap chic.

One company, the Owens-Illinois Can Company, took its stock tin ware and added Fiesta-like decals, thus expanding its market to include Fiesta buyers. Notice the different style of breadboxes shown here. Many of these decals were put on a variety of products, such as different styles of canisters.

In addition to the items pictured, a step-on garbage can and dustpan have also been discovered with these decals.

As these items were made quickly, you will notice decals that are crooked, off-center, and even ripped in half.

Tin canisters and wastebasket with decals.

Two tin breadboxes with decals.

Kitchen stool and three-tier vegetable bin.

Fiesta Mexicana Go-Along four-piece canister set in black and yellow. Sold at auction in October 2006 for **$15.**

Tin napkin holder with decals.

Two different five-piece popcorn sets. Notice the set on the top (with the turquoise individual bowl) has the familiar set of rings toward the top. The other set (with the red individual bowl) does not have rings.

TIN KITCHENWARE

Fiesta-Wood

Fiesta-Wood was another great reworking of the Homer Laughlin China Company's line. The G.H. Specialty Company of Milwaukee, Wisconsin, designed this tableware made of wood.

In 1938, the G.H. Specialty Company applied for a copyright for its Fiesta-Wood line. As you can see, the pieces were made of wood. The salad bowls are all slightly oval (not perfectly round). Each piece has the familiar band of rings in dark blue, red, yellow, and green. Some were hand painted with trees, shrubs, birds, and flowers.

The wooden relish tray has a glass insert made by the Indiana Glass Company. It is clear glass with frosted illustrations in each of the five sections. As these illustrations are hard to see, the glass insert was placed on a 9" cobalt blue lunch plate so you could see its size and also the wonderful craftsmanship.

The footed salad bowl also rests on a tray of the same size as the wooden relish base. The only difference is the size of the well that holds the piece in place.

Serving trays were also made in several sizes.

Hors d'oeuvres trays were also made by the G.H. Specialty Company. One tray had a detachable mushroom with holes to hold toothpicks. Another had a fish in the center for the same purpose.

If you can find an example, check it carefully. Many have become warped from being left in water.

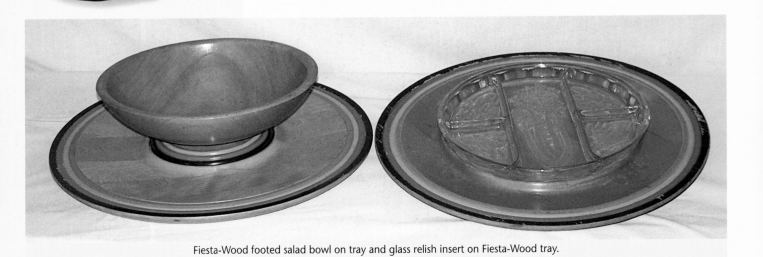

Fiesta-Wood footed salad bowl on tray and glass relish insert on Fiesta-Wood tray.

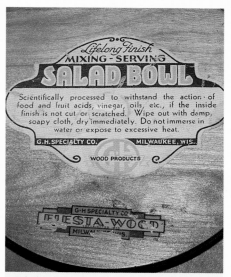

Label on bottom of Fiesta-Wood salad bowl.

Front: Fiesta-Wood tray. Back: Fiesta-Wood trays for the footed salad bowl and glass relish insert.

Glass insert for the Fiesta-Wood relish tray.

Fiesta-Wood footed salad bowl and matching tray.

Wooden Fiesta salad bowl with Fiesta colored ring base. Sold at auction in October 2006 for **$65.**

FIESTA-WOOD

New and Old Fakes and Frauds

BY MIKE CHERVENKA

Collectors of Fiesta are generally very fortunate. Unlike collectors in other fields who have been deluged with mass-produced fakes and knockoffs, there are relatively few reproduction-related problems with Fiesta.

When asked what concerns them most, many Fiesta buyers complain more about decisions made by the Homer Laughlin China Company executives than problems with fakes and reproductions. Collectors often view some company policies regarding reissues and abrupt production changes as unfriendly towards collectors.

On the positive side, though, the Homer Laughlin China Company has consistently marked the great majority of Fiesta. Beginning collectors can avoid a great deal of potential confusion and mistakes (especially if buying online) by spending a brief time learning about the various Fiesta marks.

COLORS

As most collectors are aware, there are two broad periods of Fiesta production. Production from 1936, when Fiesta was introduced, to 1969 when many of the pieces were restyled, to the end of 1972 when production stopped, is the so-called "original" period. Pieces made since Fiesta was reintroduced in February 1986 are generally referred to as "Post-'86" pieces.

One of the ways to separate original 1936-1972 pieces from Post-'86 pieces is by color. But this can get difficult. There were 14 standard production colors used during the 36 years of original production. At least 22 different colors have been produced in Post-'86 pieces. That is in addition, of course, to the 14 original colors, for a total of, at minimum, 36 colors. Include special orders and other nonstandard production runs, and the number is much higher.

All these colors can very confusing, especially when buying collectibles in online auctions. First, there is the problem of descriptions. The online auction seller cleaning out Mom's cupboards is probably going to describe a pitcher as "green" whether it's light green, medium green, or sea mist green. Photos aren't much help. Between poor photography and wide differences among computer monitors, a picture alone of the "green" pitcher may not present the color accurately. That's why marks are very important in separating original pieces from Post-'86 production, especially when buying without a first-hand examination as in an online auction.

MARKS

Marks on both original and Post-'86 pieces may be of three forms: rubber-stamped, molded below the surface, or molded above the surface. All three methods were used on both periods so the method of application has no bearing on age. The most important features of marks are the letter "F" in Fiesta, the spacing of the letters in "Fiesta," and any words that may appear with the word "Fiesta."

In original 1936 to 1972 production, the letter "F" in Fiesta closely resembles a lower case, or small, cursive letter "f." The word "Fiesta" in the original mark is very similar to how the word would look if handwritten. All the letters after the "f" flow together and are at least touching, if not smoothly interconnected. The only other words to appear in original marks are HLCo (Homer Laughlin Company), Made in USA, and Genuine. See Figs. 1, 2, 3.

Fig. 1: The basic stamped mark of original Fiesta produced from 1936 to 1972. Note that the "F" is similar to a lower case or small "f" while the Post-'86 "F" is more like an upper case or capital "F." The letters "I-E-S-T-A" are connected as if handwritten in a single word.

Fig. 2: The basic stamped marks of original 1936-1972 Fiesta vary in small details. Around 1940, for example, the word "Genuine" was added to the mark. This mark is probably the most common of all the original-period stamped marks.

Fig. 3: One of the most common original-period molded marks. Be sure to inspect all molded marks carefully. Glaze often fills in molded marks and may hide details in the "F," which are crucial to dating.

The earliest original period marks generally included "Fiesta" and "HLCo USA" only, or a Homer Laughlin Company monogram and "Made in USA." In the late 1930s Fiesta became so popular competitors were making knockoff and look-alike patterns. The company wanted to distinguish the original line, so around 1940 the word "Genuine" was added to the mark.

Beginning in 1986, the letter "F" in "Fiesta" went through a considerable transformation. A distinctive loop was added to the "F," creating the appearance of an uppercase, or capital, cursive letter "F." In printed marks, the letters forming "Fiesta" began appearing as separate, unconnected capital letters. In Post-'86 molded marks, though, letters in "Fiesta" still appear to be somewhat connected. (See Figs. 4, 5, 6.) Words found in Post-'86 marks, which never appear in original pre-1972 marks, include "Lead Free," letter date codes, and "Homer Laughlin China Co." spelled out rather than abbreviated. The trademark ™ and registration ® symbols are also found only in Post-'86 marks, never in original pre-1972 marks.

"Lead Free" and date codes began appearing in Post-'86 stamped marks in January 1992. Post-'86 Fiesta made before 1992 was not date coded.

Homer Laughlin date codes use capital letters to represent the year and month. The first year Fiesta marks included the date code was 1992. At

Fig. 4: The basic Post-'86 stamped mark used when Fiesta was brought back into production in 1986. Note the large flourishes to the top and base of the letter "F." Also note that the letters "I-E-S-T-A" are not connected and appear as separate letters.

Fig. 5: In April 1992 the new stamped mark from Fig. 1 was updated. From 1992 onward, the stamped mark included "Lead Free," the name "Homer Laughlin China Co." spelled out, and a date code. The date code shown is LLC for March 1997.

Fig. 6: The new molded Post-'86 mark is somewhat closer in appearance to marks of the original period. Note that the letter "F" is still substantially different from the original molded "F," and there is a clear break between the "E" and the "S."

that time the year code for 1992 was GG. The current code for 2007 is VV. Months are indicated by a single letter: A for January through L for December. The example shown in Fig. 5, for example, is date coded LLC, representing the year 1997, and the month of March.

Although Homer Laughlin began using date codes on commercial products in 1960, the Fiesta consumer line was not included until 1992. Stamped marks on original Fiesta made between 1960 and 1972 will not be date marked. Only pieces made from 1992 and forward carry the date codes.

While marks can be very helpful in determining age, keep in mind that the guidelines discussed here are broad, general rules. Some Fiesta, for example, was rarely or never marked, including some of the most sought-after pieces such as shakers, juice glasses, teacups, and demitasse cups. Remember, too, that molded marks are often obscured by glaze and may not show up in photos, especially those viewed on a computer monitor. Be sure to ask sellers very specific questions about marks when you can't examine pieces firsthand. Marks

Fig. 8: The molded mark on the Post-'86 JC Penney lamp is squeezed into a tight ring under the base. The compressed "F" in Fiesta has sometimes been confused with the lower case "f" in original period marks. This lamp was made in the first nine Post-'86 colors: apricot, black, cobalt blue, periwinkle blue, rose, turquoise, sea mist green, white, and yellow.

Fig. 7: This 10" lamp is often mistakenly advertised as rare in local auction and estate sale advertising. It is Post-'86 production, made exclusively for JC Penney in 1993. It may be confusing because the molded mark is somewhat similar to an original molded mark.

can help pinpoint production dates when the color can't be determined from online photos or the seller isn't acquainted with the correct company names Fiesta buyers use to describe colors.

One area of collecting where marks can only be of partial help is with the deliberate fakes that are intentionally made to deceive the buyer. The disk pitchers in Figs. 9 and 10, for example, are genuine original period Fiesta and have the appropriate markings. Looking at the marks alone in this case, though, wouldn't be enough. It's only when the entire piece is considered does each fake become obvious.

Each of the fakes is quite ambitious and fairly convincing. The red Coca-Cola slogan is a nearly perfect copy of an original Coca-Cola slogan, including the typeface of the lettering. The Roosevelt piece has also been carefully researched. The image of FDR is copied from a genuine campaign item used in 1936. Both fakes appeared at non-Fiesta sales events. The Coke pitcher showed up at a Coca-Cola auction in the early 1990s; the FDR pitcher was shown at a political collectors show in 2002. The fake Coke pitcher has also been seen in yellow and probably exists in other colors. No

Fig. 9: A genuine pre-1972 original period ivory Fiesta water pitcher with a forged advertising message. The red "Drink Coca-Cola, 5¢ glass or bottle" was applied in the mid-1990s. This is a pure fantasy item; no old counterparts exist.

other reports of the FDR pitchers have been received, but they are probably out there.

In both cases, the sellers initially thought their items were authentic. Each seller had carefully consulted reference books on Fiesta and confirmed to their satisfaction that the marks and colors were genuine. And to that extent, they were right. Both pieces are genuine original period Fiesta, but the applied images are forgeries. No records at either Coca-Cola or the Homer Laughlin China Company showed the Coke pitcher was ever produced. No reference books or factory catalogs on Coca-Cola or Fiesta ever pictured or described such a piece before the early 1990s. Likewise with the FDR pitcher. No political reference book or auction catalogs of political collections before 2002 ever included a description or photo of any similar item.

While most confusion over dating Fiesta is due to honest mistakes in separating original products from Post-'86 production, collectors still need to be wary of the occasional fake intentionally made to deceive. A healthy skepticism, which costs nothing, is always the best first defense against intentional misrepresentation.

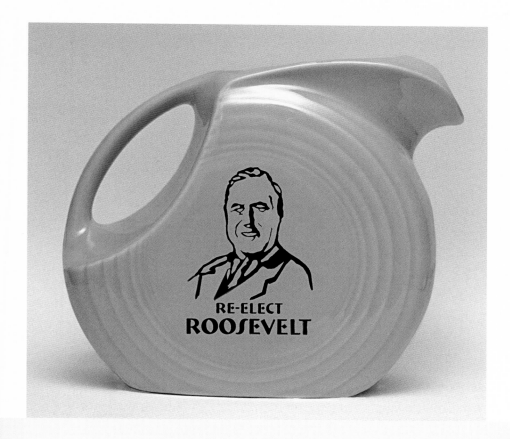

Fig. 10: Another original period disc water pitcher in yellow with a faked image, "Re-Elect Roosevelt." In this case, the artwork was copied from a genuine campaign textile. This is another fantasy item; no old counterpart ever existed.

Other Lines

None of the following four lines were intended to have Fiesta stamps, but since some styles and colors were shared, and production times overlapped, a few oddities exist. Some resources also combine the production dates for more than one line, but since each has distinct characteristics, we present them here as separate lines.

- Amberstone
- Fiesta Casuals
- Casualstone
- Fiesta Ironstone

Amberstone

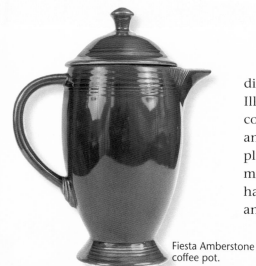

Fiesta Amberstone coffee pot.

Amberstone—in both modified and original Fiesta shapes—was distributed as part of the Sheffield line by J&H International of Wilmette, Illinois, beginning in 1967 as a grocery store promotion. The rich, coffee-color glaze can be found on 27 items, from ashtrays to vegetable bowls, and also featured a stylized scroll and shield decoration in black, mostly on plates and other flat surfaces. Some pieces were given a face-lift, such as the marmalade, which lost its flared knob and received a 1960s mushroom-type handle. The same thing happened to the knob on the covered casserole and teapot. Amberstone was produced for about two years.

DEGREE OF DIFFICULTY: 1

Fiesta Amberstone marmalade, left, and a Post-'86 standard sugar bowl in black.

Fiesta Amberstone covered butter dish.

Fiesta Amberstone place setting with 10" plate, cup and saucer, and 6" bread plate.

Fiesta Amberstone deep plate.

Fiesta Casuals

DEGREE OF DIFFICULTY: 2-3

The Fiesta Casuals line from the mid-1960s featured two patterns. The first pattern, called Yellow Carnation, consisted of yellow flowers with brown accents and leaves on a white background. The platter, plates, and saucers had a yellow band around the edge. The rest of the line was made up of yellow Fiesta. Sugar bowl, creamer, cups, fruit bowls, and nappies completed this set.

The other Fiesta Casuals pattern also consisted of flowers—turquoise with brown centers. Collectors have dubbed this pattern "Hawaiian 12-point Daisy." This design was used on white plates with a turquoise rim. It also came in the same selection of pieces as Yellow Carnation. The solid color that accompanied this design was turquoise.

Casualstone

DEGREE OF DIFFICULTY: 1

The Casualstone line from 1970 was another short-lived grocery store promotion, distributed by Coventry Ware of Barberton, Ohio, and stamped "Coventry." It has the antique gold glaze, and the plates and other flat surfaces have a stamped pattern of stylized leaves and scrolls. Again, like Amberstone, the flat pieces feature the pattern. The other items in the line are solid in color. Casualstone was made in the same 27 shapes as Amberstone. Design changes include C-handles on the cups and creamer, and a more flared knob on the lids of covered pieces.

Casualstone place setting with 10" plate, cup and saucer, and 7" plate in antique gold.

Casualstone 13" chop plate (front and back) in antique gold.

fiesta Fiesta Ironstone

In 1969, in an effort to stop declining sales, Fiesta dinnerware had to be "reinvented." New life was injected into the line by changing the colors and streamlining the shapes. Knobs and handles on many of the pieces needed to look more modern. Handles on the cup and creamer were changed from the full circle style to a C-shape style. The casserole's handles, which had been applied by hand, now became part of the mold. The knobs on top of all the pieces became more of a mushroom style rather than the familiar art deco style.

The lineup of the Fiesta Ironstone pieces that were produced from 1969-1972 were:

- Teapot
- Coffeepot
- Gravy Boat w/Liner
- Salt and Pepper Shaker
- Creamer
- Covered Sugar
- 7" Plate
- 10" Plate
- Oval Platter

- Disk Water Pitcher
- Cup and Saucer
- Coffee Mug
- Covered Casserole
- Salad Bowl
- Vegetable Bowl
- Soup/Cereal Bowl
- Dessert Bowl

DEGREE OF DIFFICULTY: 2-3

The colors of antique gold, mango red (same as original red), and turf green (olive) were put into the new line. These design updates can also be found in Amberstone and Casualstone.

Ironstone soup/cereal bowl in mango red.

Ironstone saucers in antique gold and turf green in original packaging.

Cup and saucer in turf green.

Ironstone salt and pepper shakers in antique gold and Amberstone brown.

Cup and saucer in antique gold.

Ironstone covered sugar in antique gold, and a creamer in antique gold in original packaging and with store coupon, next to a covered sugar in Amberstone.

Ironstone 7" plate, and cups in original packaging, all in turf green.

Ironstone cups in antique gold, in original packaging.

Ironstone 7" plate in turf green.

Ironstone 7" plate in antique gold.

Amberstone brown fruit/dessert bowl, and two Ironstone fruit/dessert bowls in turf green and antique gold.

Ironstone oval platter in turf green.

Ironstone 10" plate in turf green.

Ironstone sauceboat under plates in antique gold, turf green, and mango red.

Ironstone 10" plate in antique gold.

Ironstone sauceboat in turf green.

Post-'86 Fiesta

Fiesta returns

To commemorate the 50th anniversary of the debut of Fiesta, the Homer Laughlin China Company reintroduced the updated line on Feb. 28, 1986.

The original Fiesta design that had been regarded as tired and outdated in the early 1970s was now seen as ripe with nostalgic appeal. Baby boomers who grew up with the original Fiesta tableware at Grandma's house or the summer cabin bought the new Fiesta as tangible proof of these childhood memories. Its clean design and the number of special pieces available, such as vases, candleholders, and trays, also lured buyers.

Called "Post-'86" Fiesta by collectors, several of the new items are produced using vintage molds, including the two larger sizes of the disk pitchers, sugar/creamer/tray set, tripod and round candleholders, C-handle creamer, sauceboat, 8" vase, and salt and pepper shakers.

As with the vintage line, the Homer Laughlin China Company also licenses several companies to produce coordinating items for Post-'86 Fiesta, including cutlery, drawer pulls, glassware, kitchen timers, linens, and even message boards.

Homer Laughlin China Company continues to introduce new colors and items to the line, so check with local retailers.

Spoon rest in sunflower.

Carafe and four tumblers in chartreuse.

Fiesta colors produced since 1986

APRICOT—moderate, pale pinkish-orange (discontinued in 1998)

BLACK—(introduced in 1986)

CHARTREUSE—yellowish-green, more yellow than the original (produced from 1997 to 1999)

CINNABAR—burgundy or maroon (introduced in 2000)

COBALT BLUE—dark navy (introduced in 1986)

EVERGREEN—dark green (introduced in 2007)

HEATHER—medium purple (introduced in 2006)

JUNIPER—dark forest green, almost a bluish green (produced from 1999 to 2001)

LILAC—pastel purple or violet (produced from 1993 to 1995)

PEACOCK—bright bluish-green (introduced in 2005)

PEARL GRAY—similar to vintage gray, more luminous (produced from 1999 to 2001)

PERIWINKLE—grayish-blue (produced from 1989 to 2006)

PERSIMMON—dark orange-red; coral (introduced in 1995)

PLUM—deep purple (introduced in 2002)

ROSE—bubblegum pink (produced from 1986 to 2005)

SAPPHIRE—royal blue (sold only by Bloomingdale's in 1996 and 1997)

SCARLET—bright red (introduced in 2004)

SEA MIST GREEN—pastel, light green (produced from 1991 to 2005)

SHAMROCK—dark, grassy green (introduced in 2002)

SUNFLOWER—bright, rich yellow (introduced in 2001)

TANGERINE—bright orange (introduced in 2003)

TURQUOISE—greenish-blue (introduced in 1988)

WHITE—(introduced in 1986)

YELLOW—pale yellow (produced from 1987 to 2002)

Post-'86 items

BOWLS:

PIE BAKER, (#417) 6-3/8", (#419) 8-1/4", and (#487) 10-1/4"; three sizes of round pie-shaped containers, which can be used in the oven for pies, desserts, quiches, and more.

BOUILLON CUP (#450), 6-3/4 ounces; a great little cup with a variety of uses from holding sake to Jello and fruit cups to vegetable dip. Not part of the original line. This item made its debut in February 1986.

CEREAL, STACKING (#472), 6-1/2", 11 ounces; a larger version of the 5-3/8" fruit bowl.

FRUIT BOWL (#459), 5-3/8", 6-1/4 ounces; similar to the Fiesta ironstone soup/cereal bowl.

CHILI BOWL (#098), 18 ounces; as the name implies, it was designed by HLC to hold chili. Also great for individual baked desserts, such as apple crisp.

CHOWDER (#576); extra large, two quarts.

GUSTO BOWL (#723), 23 ounces; slightly larger and wider than the chili bowl, this utilitarian piece is great for dips, sauces, candy, or nuts.

BOWL, SMALL (#460), 5-5/8", 14-1/4 ounces.

BOWL, MEDIUM (#461), 6-7/8", 19 ounces.

BOWL, LARGE (#471), 8-1/4", 40 ounces.

BOWL, EXTRA LARGE (#455), 80 ounces; this piece is modeled after the nappy design from vintage Fiesta. It is interesting to note that Homer Laughlin China Company makes four sizes of this bowl in the same basic style. The company is listening to what consumers and retailers want. Regardless of what size family the consumer has, there is a basic serving bowl to fit their needs.

MEOW BOWL, 8 ounces.

MIXING, BOWL, SMALL (#421), 7-1/2", 44 ounces.

MIXING, BOWL, MEDIUM (#422), 8-1/2", 60 ounces.

MIXING, BOWL, LARGE (#482), 9-1/2", 70 ounces; great for mixing and serving. These three mixing bowls comprise a smaller set than the vintage Fiesta seven-piece mixing bowl set.

PEDESTAL BOWL (#765), 9-7/8", 64 ounces; designed to be used as a centerpiece container, this piece is a catch-all bowl that can also be used for serving.

PASTA (#462), 12", 21 ounces; based on the vintage rim soup bowl; by enlarging the piece, it is now put to multiple uses. The 12" pasta bowl has been used in gourmet restaurants for single servings of pasta or salad. Its presentation is great.

RIM SOUP BOWL (#451), 9", 13-1/4 ounces.

Post-'86 items

BREAD TRAY (#412), 12" by 5-3/4". With the rise in popularity of bread machines and supermarkets expanding their bread offerings, this is a useful piece. Not too many other tableware manufacturers include one in their lines.

CANDLESTICKS, PYRAMID (#489), 3-1/2". Part of the original 1986 reintroduction, these candlesticks were produced from vintage molds. They were discontinued around 2001.

CANDLESTICKS, ROUND (#488), 3-5/8". Also part of the original 1986 reintroduction line. Round candlesticks, like the pyramid candlesticks, are also made from the original molds.

CANISTER, SMALL (#571), one quart, 7-3/8"

CANISTER, MEDIUM (#572), two quarts, 8-1/2"

CANISTER, LARGE (#573), three quarts, 9-3/4"

CARAFE (#448) with handle, 60 ounces. This piece, updated from the original, is different in several ways. First, the new carafe has no top. Second, the body is not round like the older model. Third, the newer model has no foot. Also, there is a line of rings toward the top of the newer piece, unlike the vintage one, which had rings at its foot.

COVERED BUTTER (#494), 7-1/8" long. This item was not in the original Fiesta line. Collectors have embraced it by combining it with their vintage pieces.

COVERED CASSEROLE (#495), 70 ounces. Great for keeping vegetables hot at the table, this piece changed greatly from the original version, which debuted in 1936. It was revamped in 1969 and then restyled again in 1986. The newest casserole (the third styling in the Fiesta line) lost its handles, thus giving it a more streamlined appearance. The finial was also changed back to the style of the original one.

COVERED SUGAR, INDIVIDUAL (#498), 8-3/4 ounces. The Fiesta line of today boasts two sugars and creamers. This one is sold by itself (hence the name "individual"), while the other is sold as a set (complete with tray). The individual sugar is made from the original marmalade mold.

CREAMER, INDIVIDUAL (#492), 7 ounces. This piece was made from the 1967 restyled creamer mold.

CUP, AFTER DINNER (#476) (demitasse), 3 ounces.

Round candleholders in black.

Original Post-'86 demitasse cup and saucer in yellow (redesigned in 2001), and mini disk pitcher in black with trial decal.

SAUCER, AFTER DINNER (#477) (demitasse), 5 ounces. Another crossover from the vintage Fiesta line, the Post-'86 after dinner cup and saucer have already been discontinued. They were replaced with after dinner cup #549. For whatever reason, Homer Laughlin China Company never reissued the demitasse coffeepot.

CUP, AFTER DINNER (#549), 3 ounces. This style replaced the stick-handle (#476) variety.

CUP (#452) 7-3/4 ounces.

SAUCER (#470), 6". This saucer is basically the same style as the version introduced in 1936. The handle on the cup was changed from the ring style to the current "C" style in 1967. Other minor revisions include the foot of the cup; some may be slightly thicker or heavier than others. Cups also lost their inside rings over the years.

CUP, JUMBO (#149), 18 ounces.

SAUCER, JUMBO (#293), 6-3/4". This twosome is one of many pieces that were borrowed from other Homer Laughlin China Company lines. The cup probably holds more coffee than the surgeon general would recommend any one person to consume in a 24-hour period. The jumbo cup is great for holding candy or nuts. It's also wonderful for chili or soup as you can either use it like a bowl and eat the soup with a spoon, or use the cup's handle and drink the soup.

DISC PITCHER, MINIATURE (#475), 5 ounces.

DISC PITCHER, SMALL (#485), 28 ounces.

DISC PITCHER, LARGE (#484), 67 ounces. Both the small and large disc pitchers are made from original molds. The miniature version is a scaled-down version of its larger siblings. Back in the 1930s, novelty creamers were all the rage, and many companies manufactured them. Many collectors today use the miniature disc pitcher to hold cream for coffee, but it can also be used as an individual bud vase at each place setting.

HOSTESS TRAY (#753), 12-1/4" diameter. Slightly larger than the round serving tray, this piece, when accompanied by a smaller Fiesta bowl, makes a great chip and dip or salsa set.

MUGS (#453), 10-1/4 ounce. Based on the old Tom and Jerry mug design, this cup is a great addition to the collection of any person "even a non-Fiesta collector" who drinks coffee or tea.

MUG, JAVA (#570), 12 ounces. Slightly larger than the 10-3/4 ounces variety, this piece was designed for people with large hands.

MUG, CAPPUCCINO (#418), 21 ounces. As the name implies, this item was designed with plenty of room for foaming milk.

MUG, PEDESTAL (#424), 18 ounces. This is a fun mug for sipping any type of hot drink, from cappuccino to coffee with flavored creamers, spices, and/or liquor.

OVAL SERVING BOWL, DEEP (#409), 12", 52 ounces. An open vegetable bowl was a staple in almost all dinnerware lines. This version, with its oval shape, adds interest to any table when combined with other round Fiesta items, such as plates, bowls, casseroles, etc.

PLANTER/SAUCER SET (#859): two pieces, planter, 3-5/8" by 6"; saucer, 7" diameter.

PLATE, BREAD AND BUTTER (#463), 6-1/8".

PLATE, SALAD (#464), 7-1/4".

PLATE, LUNCHEON (#465), 9".

PLATE, DINNER (#466), 10-1/2". New, slightly larger molds were made for the plates. Vintage bread and butter, salad, and luncheon plates are actually larger than Post-'86 counterparts due to shrinkage in the current firing process. The old and new dinner plates are almost identical in size.

PLATE, CHOP (#467), 11-3/4". An all-purpose platter that matched the plates line for line. This Post-'86 piece is approximately 3/4" smaller than its vintage sibling.

PLATE, PIZZA (#505), 15". A great addition for any pizza lover in your life, this piece has no vintage mate. Completely flat except for the lip, this 15" variety will hold any pizza from one delivered to your home to one right out of your oven.

PLATE, WELLED SNACK (#760), 10-1/2". Based on designs from the 1930s and 1940s, this plate is all the rage for hostesses to provide to their guests. Put a cup in the well, fill the plate with food, and you can move around the room while eating and socializing. A bouillon cup can also be added to turn this into a shrimp and cocktail sauce server.

PLATTER (#456), 9-5/8".

PLATTER (#457), 11-5/8".

PLATTER (#458), 13-5/8". For the Post-'86 Fiesta line, Homer Laughlin China Company introduced three oval platters. Platters #456 and #457 are smaller than the vintage Fiesta platter, while platter #458 is an inch bigger than its 1930s counterpart.

RAMEKIN (#568) 4" by 2", 8 ounces. Thanks to Martha Stewart and the Food Network, many Americans are purchasing ramekins to make their own individual flans or custards.

Salt and pepper shakers in chartreuse.

Two-cup teapot in chartreuse.

SERVING TRAY, ROUND (#468) 11". The round serving tray is a perfect piece for serving cakes, tarts, or cheese and crackers.

SHAKER, SALT (#750), 2-5/8".

SHAKER, PEPPER (#751), 2-5/8". Another staple in dinnerware lines. The Post-'86 collection has two sets of salt and pepper shakers. This set is made from vintage molds and is placed on the table for use during a meal.

SPOON REST (#439), 8". Designed for the Post-'86 line, this latecomer wasn't added until approximately 2001. Great for the top of the stove to catch drips and spills—and for reminding you where you put the ladle.

SUGAR AND CREAMER SET (#821). Made from the same molds that were used in the promotional campaign, this set seems to sell well. Because of the clay used, these Post-'86 pieces are somewhat lighter in weight.

SUGAR PACKET HOLDER (#479). This item was brought into the Fiesta line from a Homer Laughlin China Company restaurant pattern. Glazed in the current Fiesta colors, it holds packets of sugar and sugar substitutes.

TEAPOT, 2-CUP (#764). Perfect for tea for one or for a tea party with a favorite doll, this teapot allows the owner to brew only a small batch of tea at one time.

TEAPOT, COVERED (#496), 44 ounces. A redesign of the original eight-cup teapot, this size holds approximately 5-1/2 cups. With all the recently discussed benefits of green tea, teapots like this are on the rise in popularity.

TRIVET (#443). A handy item, this trivet with an embossed Fiesta senorita is perfect for holding hot pans during mealtime.

TUMBLER (#446), 6-1/2 ounces. Sold either individually or in sets, this tumbler has been paired with the juice pitcher in special promotions.

UTENSIL CROCK (#447), 6-5/8". With the renewed interest in gourmet cooking, a utensil crock is a perfect item for kitchen counters. With its wide-mouth design, it can easily hold whips, spatulas, and spoons galore.

VASE, BUD (#490), 6".

VASE, SMALL (#440), 8".

VASE, MEDIUM (#491), 9-5/8". All three vases are slightly smaller then their 1930s counterparts. So far no 12" vase is being produced.

VASE, ROYALTY (#565), 7-1/2". A unique design, this vase bows out toward the bottom.

VASE, MONARCH (#566), 9-1/2". Approximately the same height as the medium vase (#491), the monarch vase's ring pattern styling seems better suited to the Fiesta line than any of the vintage varieties.toward the bottom.

Millennium I vase in yellow.

Place setting with 10" plate, 7" plate and cup and saucer in lilac.

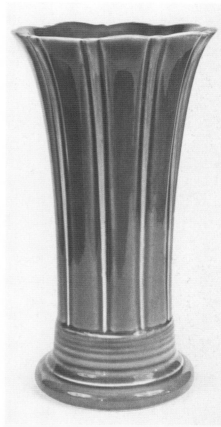

10" vase in lilac.

Three Post-'86 pitchers—disk juice pitcher, disk water pitcher, and mini pitcher—in lilac.

Tom & Jerry mug in lilac.

fiesta

Fiesta advertising plate, 12" diameter chop, with mango red logo and type.

Bouillon cups in black and white.

Tripod candleholders in black and white.

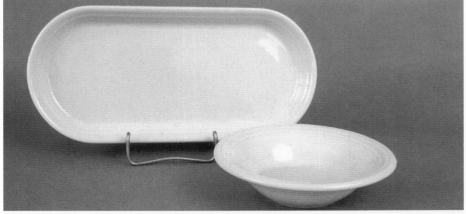

Bread tray and cereal bowl in yellow.

Standard sugar bowl and Fiesta Mates 5 ounces creamer in black.

Napkin ring set in persimmon.

Millennium III vase in persimmon.

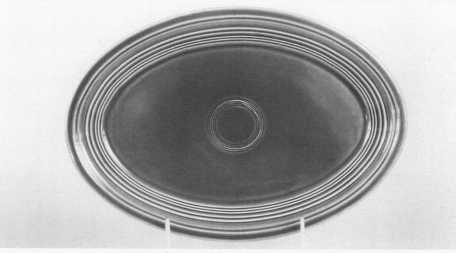

Large platter (13-1/2" wide) in cobalt blue.

Millennium II vase in turquoise.

Round serving tray in sapphire.

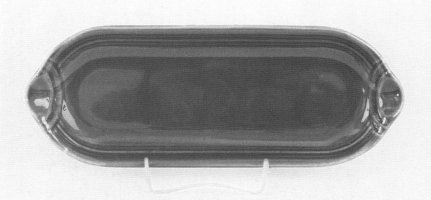

Relish or utility in sapphire.

5-1/2 cup teapot in black and 2-cup teapot in persimmon (note difference in handles).

Trivets in cobalt blue and sunflower.

Range shakers in persimmon on a figure-8 tray.

Fruit bowl in chartreuse.

Two sizes of pie bakers in persimmon and turquoise.

fiesta

Two-quart extra large bowl in pearl gray.

Two smaller platters in turquoise and chartreuse.

Soup bowl in cobalt blue and cereal bowl in periwinkle.

Deep plates in turquoise and apricot.

Chili bowl in persimmon.

Commemorative presentation bowl sitting on an upside-down hostess bowl, both in persimmon, forming a large compote.

Vases: two 8" in cinnabar (left) and turquoise, and a 10" in juniper.

Sugar and creamer on figure-8 tray in turquoise.

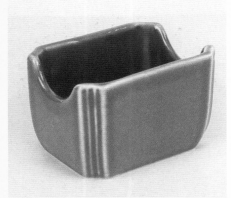

Sugar packet holder in lilac.

Covered casserole in apricot.

Pizza tray in persimmon with glaze flaw.

Hostess tray in turquoise.

Sauceboat in lilac.

Chop plate in lilac.

Covered butter dish in lilac.

Large oval platter in lilac.

Soup bowl and cereal bowl in lilac.

8-1/4" serving bowl in sapphire.

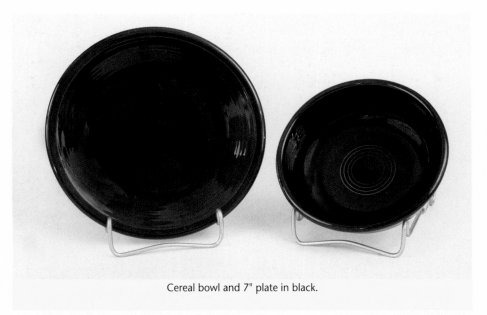

Cereal bowl and 7" plate in black.

7" plate and soup bowl ,10" plate, and cup and saucer in sapphire.

Bud vases in pearl gray, lilac, plum, juniper, and cobalt blue.

Jumbo mug and saucer in turquoise.

Bud vases in yellow, white, sea mist, apricot, and sunflower.

Bud vases in cinnabar, chartreuse, persimmon, turquoise, and black.

fiesta

Close-up showing Fiesta 2000 logo and Fiesta 2000 round platter, 14-1/2" diameter, and luncheon plate in pearl gray.

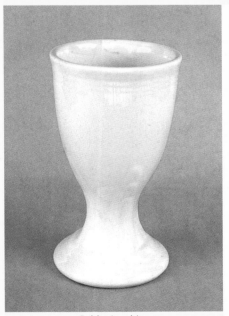

Goblet in white.

Fiesta 2000 10" dinner plate in persimmon, and the all-purpose bowl in cobalt blue.

Tom & Jerry mugs in persimmon, white, pearl gray, lilac, juniper, and turquoise. The turquoise mug on the bottom left is also called the "fan" or "horizon" mug.

Tom & Jerry mug in persimmon, 60th anniversary.

Tom & Jerry mugs in chartreuse, sunflower, shamrock, plum, sea mist, rose, and cinnabar.

fiesta

Disk water pitcher in white with Mickey Mouse.

Warner Bros. pie baker in yellow.

Child's set, including tumbler, bowl, and 9" plate with Noah's Ark decal.

"My First Fiesta" set, including 2-cup teapot in yellow, two ring-handle cups with saucers in periwinkle and rose, two 6" plates in yellow, and a creamer and covered sugar in turquoise; with original box.

Smiling face 9" plate in sunflower.

Warner Bros. deep plate in rose.

Bud vase in cobalt blue with floral decal, and a tumbler in black with the "Moon Over Miami" decal.

Three sizes of mixing bowls in juniper.

Three sizes of mixing bowls in chartreuse (note color variation).

White disk juice pitcher with "Sun Porch" decal, and white tumbler with "Mexicana" decal.

1999 Christmas ornaments in white and persimmon decorated and signed by former Homer Laughlin art director Jonathan Parry (1948-2000).

Tool crocks in sunflower and juniper.

Pedestal bowl in cobalt blue.

Ramekins in apricot, shamrock, cobalt blue, and cinnabar.

Welled snack plate in juniper with a white bouillon cup.

Gusto bowl in sunflower.

Medium bowl and ramekin in shamrock.

Platter in turquoise.

Latte mugs in persimmon and pearl gray. They are also known as pedestal mugs.

Left, cappuccino mug in cinnabar; right, latte mug in pearl gray.

Tripod bowls in chartreuse and juniper.

Fiesta clock in chartreuse, sold for only a matter of months by JC Penney. The clock was later produced in various colors and sold in various retail stores.

Striped Fiesta

Fiesta pieces with stripes came in two styles. The first style appeared near the beginning of production in 1936 and features three concentric rings. These were applied with glaze, so they wear very well. Almost all of the examples that have been found have red stripes on ivory. These are very hard to find. An even rarer few have been reported in ivory with cobalt blue stripes.

Discoveries so far include nested mixing bowls, 5-3/4" fruit bowls, both size nappies, 6", 7", and 9" plates, cups, saucers, salt and pepper shakers, cream soup bowls, covered casseroles, bud vases, 10" flower vases, sugar bowls and lids, demitasse cups and saucers, covered onion soup bowls, mustard jars, and relish trays. Because of the rarity of these items, expect to pay three to five times as much for Fiesta with underglazed stripes.

The second style is part of the cake set sold by Sears in the 1940s. This style was produced on 7" and 10" Fiesta plates. A set consisted of a 10" plate (for a cake or other dessert) and a service of either four or eight 7" plates. Expect to find green or maroon stripes on ivory or yellow plates. Because the stripes were painted after the plate was fired, they do not wear well, and the plates often look very worn. Collectors have not embraced this style the way they have the earlier style.

Striped plates sold as part of cake sets by Sears, circa 1937: 7" plates in green on yellow and maroon on yellow; 10" and 7" plates in green on ivory.

Saucer and 7" plate with three blue stripes.

6" plate and 5 1/2" fruit bowl with red stripes.

Commemoratives & Souvenirs

fiesta

As with any group of collecting enthusiasts, the Homer Laughlin China Collectors Association holds annual conferences and issues commemorative pieces to mark the occasions. Formed in 1998 as an all-volunteer, member-operated organization, HLCCA is dedicated to providing education and communication for all those interested in the wares of the Homer Laughlin China Company, from 1873 to the present. *The Dish*, the official publication of HLCCA, is published quarterly.

Presentation bowl in cobalt blue, gilded for use as the HLCCA exhibition Grand Award and bearing a facsimile of Jonathan Parry's signature, presented to Fred Mutchler.

Homer Laughlin Fiesta souvenir plate, 6-1/4" diameter.

Disk water pitchers in cobalt blue, presented as HLCCA awards to Fred Mutchler in 1999 and 2000, each with a facsimile of the signature of Frederick H. Rhead, original designer of the Fiesta line.

Homer Laughlin China Collector's Association disk juice pitchers: The 1933 zeppelin motif was issued in 2001; the 1934 ship design was issued in 2002.

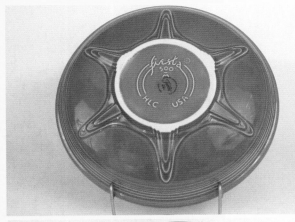

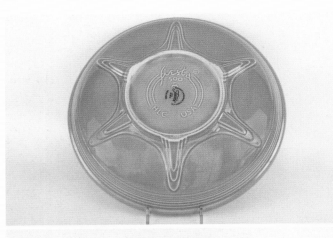

Top and bottom of presentation bowl (in persimmon) marking the 500,000,000th piece of Fiesta.

Top and bottom of presentation bowl (in chartreuse) marking the 500,000,000th piece of Fiesta.

Right, 2001 HLCCA Silver Award in a Fiesta disk juice pitcher in pearl gray; left, 2002 HLCCA Gold Award in a disk water pitcher in cobalt blue.

White tool crock and small pie baker with Homer Laughlin China Collector's Association 2002 Conference decals.

50th anniversary (1986) ring-handle mugs, 3-1/4" tall, in white, each having the anniversary sticker.

fiesta

Fiesta 60th anniversary beverage set: disk water pitcher and four tumblers in sapphire, all with the anniversary mark, sold by Bloomingdale's.

Fiesta 60th anniversary beverage set: disk water pitcher and four tumblers in lilac, all with the anniversary mark. This set was also produced in periwinkle, rose, persimmon, cobalt blue, and turquoise.

Fiesta Club of America round serving tray in chartreuse from 1998. This group was active from 1995 to 1999.

Homer Laughlin China Collector's Association disk juice pitchers: The 1930 Chrysler Building pitcher was issued in 1999.

Homer Laughlin China Collector's Association disk juice pitchers: The 1931 Dick Tracy pitcher was issued in 2000; the 1932 radio pitcher was also issued in 2001.

Fiesta Go-Alongs

Collectors who can never get enough of their favorite collectibles have coined the term "go-alongs," which refers to items made to coordinate with Fiesta colors. In this case, Fiesta enthusiasts search for anything unique and different to add to their collections. Their passion has led to many great discoveries.

For Fiesta fanatics, items as varied as cloth, food labels, seed packets, silverware, glassware, egg cookers, and even bun warmers add excitement to the hunt.

This raffia-wrapped metal handle fits a #2 mixing bowl, turning it into an ice bucket.

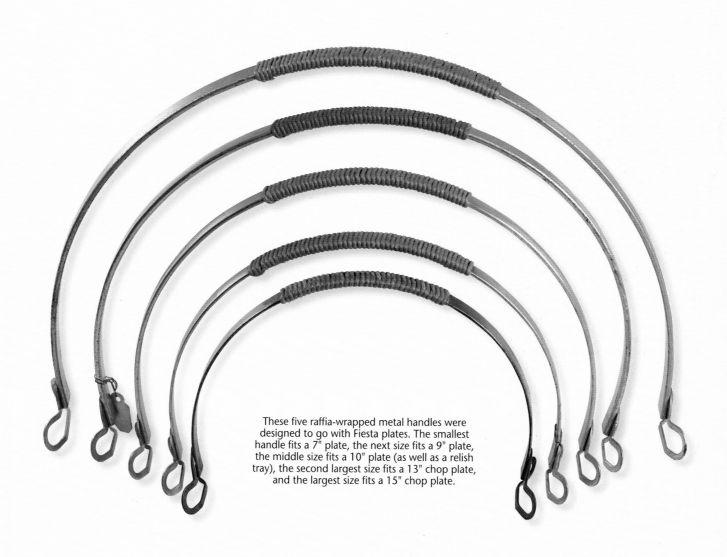

These five raffia-wrapped metal handles were designed to go with Fiesta plates. The smallest handle fits a 7" plate, the next size fits a 9" plate, the middle size fits a 10" plate (as well as a relish tray), the second largest size fits a 13" chop plate, and the largest size fits a 15" chop plate.

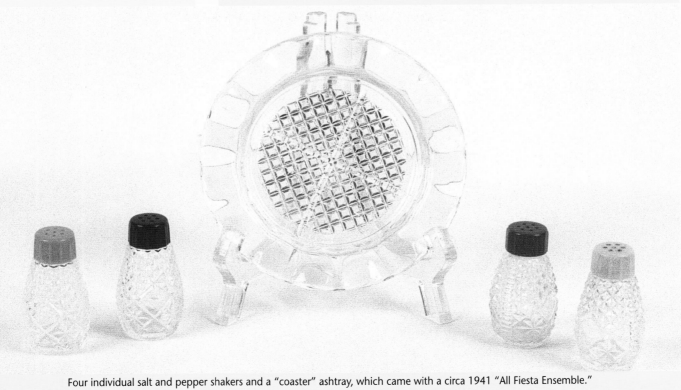

Four individual salt and pepper shakers and a "coaster" ashtray, which came with a circa 1941 "All Fiesta Ensemble."

Go-along glassware with banded tops. **$10-$15 each**

Go-along glassware with Mexican motifs referred to as the cactus, pot, and sombrero. **$15-$20 each**

A collection of go-along utensils made by Sta-Brite Corp., New Haven, Connecticut, with color-matched handles; the blue handles often turn a purple-black hue.

Fiesta Go-Along glass water pitcher and six tumblers with Fiesta colored stripes, new in box. Sold at auction in October 2006 for **$10.**

Flatware with colorful handles. Styles such as this were shipped along with glassware and Fiesta dinnerware from Homer Laughlin. See page 253 for a copy of an original advertisement.

Go-along glassware from the original four-place ensemble in 1939, also called "the dancing lady" ensemble because it includes the only appearance on glass of the Fiesta dancing lady. Rare. **$60-$70 each**

Front and back of a Fiesta promotional poster, circa 1936, showing what may be the first appearance of the dancing lady that became part of the line's logo.

fiesta

Fiesta brochures.